The Bangladesh Garment Industry and the Global Supply Chain

This book analyzes the choices and constraints of management within the Bangladesh garment industry and how management negotiates these challenges to ensure that the global garment supply chain is sustainable.

Exploring the international South Asian garment industry and using middle management and the owners of Bangladeshi factories as a case study, the book assesses the limits and costs of globalization for Bangladesh, and outlines the challenges of the fast-fashion business model for the global market. It focusses on the changing dynamics of the entrepreneur class, how they manage factories and their experiences with Accord-Alliance, and the challenges of sustainability. Within these four broader themes, the author critically examines management strategies towards compliance and labour productivity, transnational governance, buyer–supplier relationships, and power dynamics. This book is the first to explore management's perceptions of workers, buyers, and government through an analysis of four factories which demonstrate the role of mid-level management, how supervisors treat production workers, workers' impact on innovation, welfare programmes as well as CSR policies, and the impact of COVID-19.

Offering new perspectives on Bangladesh's garment export industry, this book will be of interest to researchers in the field of policy studies, labour studies, South and South-East Asian studies, development studies, international trade, and political science.

Shahidur Rahman is Professor in the Department of Economics and Social Sciences, School of Humanities and Social Sciences at BRAC University, Bangladesh.

Routledge Contemporary South Asia Series

133 **Labour, Global Supply Chains, and the Garment Industry in South Asia**
Bangladesh After Rana Plaza
Sanchita Banerjee Saxena

134 **Ethnic Inequality in the Northeastern Indian Borderlands**
Social Structures and Symbolic Violence
Anita Lama

135 **Kashmir and the Future of South Asia**
Edited by Sugata Bose and Ayesha Jalal

136 **Bangladesh and International Law**
Edited by Mohammad Shahabuddin

137 **Terrorism and the US Drone Attacks in Pakistan**
Killing First
Imdad Ullah

138 **The Bangladesh Garment Industry and the Global Supply Chain**
Choices and Constraints of Management
Shahidur Rahman

139 **Globalising Everyday Consumption in India**
History and Ethnography
Edited by Bhaswati Bhattacharya and Henrike Donner

For the full list of titles in the series please visit: https://www.routledge.com/Routledge-Contemporary-South-Asia-Series/book-series/RCSA

The Bangladesh Garment Industry and the Global Supply Chain

Choices and Constraints of Management

Shahidur Rahman

Routledge
Taylor & Francis Group
LONDON AND NEW YORK

First published 2021
by Routledge
2 Park Square, Milton Park, Abingdon, Oxon OX14 4RN

and by Routledge
605 Third Avenue, New York, NY 10158

Routledge is an imprint of the Taylor & Francis Group, an informa business

British Library Cataloguing-in-Publication Data
A catalogue record for this book is available from the British Library

Library of Congress Cataloging-in-Publication Data
Names: Rahman, Shahidur, author.
Title: The Bangladesh garment industry and the global supply chain : choices and constraints of management / Shahidur Rahman.
Description: Abingdon, Oxon ; New York, NY : Routledge, 2021. | Series: Routledge contemporary South Asia series | Includes bibliographical references and index.
Identifiers: LCCN 2020056391 | ISBN 9780367709693 (hardback) | ISBN 9781003153238 (ebook)
Subjects: LCSH: Clothing trade—Bangladesh. | Clothing workers—Bangladesh. | Economic development—Bangladesh. | Bangladesh—Commerce.
Classification: LCC HD9940.B362 R3449 2021 | DDC 338.4/7687095492—dc23
LC record available at https://lccn.loc.gov/2020056391

ISBN: 978-0-367-70969-3 (hbk)
ISBN: 978-0-367-72052-0 (pbk)
ISBN: 978-1-003-15323-8 (ebk)

Typeset in Times New Roman
by codeMantra

To my Son, Adipto Rahman
My Superman

Contents

List of figures ix
List of tables xi
List of boxes xiii
Preface xv
Acknowledgements xix
Glossary xxi

1 From least developed to lower-middle-income country 1

2 From million to billion-dollar industry 13

3 From first-generation to second-generation entrepreneurs 34

4 Case study: small garment factory 50

5 Case study: medium and large factory 65

6 Transnational governance: Accord and Alliance 82

7 Challenges of sustainability 100

8 Road ahead 127

Bibliography 135
Index 145

Figures

2.1 Snapshot of Bangladesh garment industry 19
7.1 Flowchart for stimulus package 125

Tables

1.1	Changes in GDP growth (in percentages)	6
1.2	Share of major sectors to GDP, 1972–2019 (in percentages)	6
1.3	Impact of five pillars of development	9
2.1	Growth of garments industry and employment	20
2.2	Distribution of major clients based on factory size	21
2.3	RMG exports of Bangladesh	21
2.4	Changing wage structure: 2006–2018	32
4.1	Profile of Texphin	57
4.2	Labour standard of small factories	61
5.1	Labour relations of IMPTX and FRA	67
7.1	How often did the following situations occur in the factory?	115
7.2	Different upgrading projects in RMG	118
7.3	Perception of buyers on the crisis	123

Boxes

2.1 Timeline of the Bangladesh RMG 15
2.2 Leading buyers of Bangladesh RMG 22
2.3 A female union leader's views on female leadership role 27
2.4 Workers' outcome standards 31
3.1 Transforming traditions: Ananta Group 43
5.1 A supervisor's tale 69
7.1 Audit experience of a factory compliance manager 109
7.2 Buyer-supplier relationship: Buyer's CSR managers' response 115
7.3 Management experience of HER project 119

Preface

By many measures, the Bangladesh export-oriented garment industry has performed enormously well over the last forty years. From a less than a million-dollar industry in the early 1980s, it became a billion-dollar industry in 2000, and over the next twenty years, the export earning has increased to $30 billion, accounting for 11% of GDP and 80% of exports. Depending on the hard work of more than 4 million workers, of whom 80% are women, Bangladesh is now the second-largest exporter of garments, behind China. With favourable government policy as well as supportive global trade arrangements, the garment owners have played a pivotal role in the rapid development of the ready-made garment (RMG) industry in this impoverished country. The socio-economic achievement in Bangladesh, however, also came with a very real price, one that resulted in the Rana Plaza collapse – the worst industrial tragedy of the world, taking the lives of more than 1,100 workers. The export-oriented garment industry was at stake because of this catastrophe, and the sustainability of this sector was uncertain. The local and global stakeholders placed enormous pressure on the government of Bangladesh, in general, and the garment entrepreneurs, in particular, to come up with a proactive action to change the culture of "business as usual" and demanded a paradigm shift in compliance. Consequentially, the sector has regained the confidence of global brands and retailers by addressing workplace safety effectively and transparently. The factory management, in collaboration with different key agents, has embraced several initiatives to ensure the sustainability of the Bangladesh RMG industry. There has been a positive impact of these initiatives on the sector and as a result, the export earning has been increased. However, the sustainability of the industry was again challenged by COVID-19, a global pandemic that has shattered the global economy. The garment owners have invested a momentous effort in overcoming the disaster caused by the pandemic.

Against this backdrop, this book, emphasizes, from a management context, the choices and constraints of the management of the export-oriented garment industry of Bangladesh in the global supply chain. The economy of the country has been transformed, mainly because of the garment industry, and the garment factory owners are the driving force of this change, along with the workers. The following aspects of factory management are presented in this book: (1) changes of the socio-economic characteristics of the entrepreneurs, (2) how they manage the factory, (3) their perceptions of transnational governance, (4) the nature of the challenges they face in doing business – ranging from the old issue of a fair price to the current pandemic situation – and how these managers ensure sustainability. Within these four broader themes, this book critically analyzes governance, management practices, buyer–supplier relationships, supply chain production, and power dynamics. This analysis will help us understanding the choices and constraints of management and how they negotiate with these challenges in the global supply chain.

What is missing in the current literature is limited study on the role played by the garment entrepreneurs in the development of the Bangladesh RMG and managements' perceptions of the overall changes that have taken place in the industry. Listening to managements' views regarding the opportunities and constraints for sustainable value chains is imperative since they execute different initiatives in the factories offered by different stakeholders (Gereffi and Lee 2016). They are the actors who are held responsible for not maintaining global labour standards. The reason why they fail or succeed is explored by incorporating their opinions. From the context of Bangladesh, there is another reason to study managers' concerns because perception varies very little between the owners and the government due to their close association with the political elite. So, the book gives an opportunity to understand the patronization of the state in the development of the industry. The method of recognizing managements' approach also creates a space in which to comprehend what the suppliers contemplate of their buyers and how they deal with global brands and retailers in this buyer-driven industry.

The book is mainly based on four case studies of Bangladeshi garment factories – one was conducted as part of my doctoral dissertation in 2004–2005, and three come from one of my research projects on "Changes in governance after Rana Plaza" in 2016–2018. Some data was used from a management survey of 152 factories in the same research project. The findings of another research project on "Scaling Matters" in 2018–2019 are also incorporated to understand the sustainability of upgrading initiatives in the factory. This updated primary data has strengthened the concentration of the book in several chapters.

The book contains eight chapters. To understand the rise and growth of the Bangladesh RMG relying on the emergence of a new capitalist class, Chapter 1 presents the economic history of the country. This chapter demonstrates that the development path of Bangladesh had been shattered during the British colonial period and Pakistan regime. Since independence of the country in 1971, there was a very slow progress of development but the the economy has started to transform since the 1990s by embracing export-led trade policy. In the migration from a Least Developed country to a Lower-Middle-Income country, the contribution of five areas cannot be denied – population control; self-sufficiency in agriculture; the role of NGOs in microfinance; remittance from low-skilled migrants; and, above all, the RMG industry.

The emphasis of Chapter 2 is the history and structure of the Bangladesh RMG industry. This chapter tells us a story of the collaboration of one local private garment business, Desh Company, with a South Korean company, Daewoo, and how crucial this collaboration was in terms of accessing the global apparel markets as well as the impact of the Multi-Fibre Agreement (MFA) on the origin of this industry. It presents the structure of this sector, contributions to the economy, and how the inception of the garment industry has changed the position of women in society. Despite these positive economic and social impacts, the workers have become vulnerable in different ways after joining the garment factories, as is evident in the collapse of Rana Plaza. This sad event is considered a hidden cost of the development of the Bangladesh garment industry.

The objective of Chapter 3 is to get an idea of the changes in ownership structure. A primary emphasis is on the differences between first-generation owners and second-generation entrepreneurs. This chapter explores how the nature of entrepreneurship has changed over time. While the first-generation owners came from a diverse background with no prior experience in this sector, the second-generation entrepreneurs joined family businesses enthusiastically and in some cases unhappily after completing higher education from overseas. This chapter also sheds light on the key source of the power of the Bangladesh garment entrepreneurs. There has been a patron-client relationship between state and business associations.

Chapter 4 showcases two case studies of small garment factories – a story of the rise, growth, and demise of a compliant factory, and the growth and struggles of a non-compliant small factory in the global supply chain. The first factory started up in 1990, believing that the basic rights of workers for a safe and healthy work environment are as important as corporate productivity and profitability. The closure of the company in 2005 leads me to study the company's fatal vulnerability after almost a decade of prosperous growth. The second case study is about a non-compliant firm that has been struggling for a long time to be sustainable in the global market. This case study focusses on the journey of a small businessman, the relationship between workers and management of a subcontracting firm, and challenges to sustain the business.

Chapter 5 presents two case studies of a medium and a large factory, respectively, where it is believed that, in an increasingly resource-constrained world, sustainable business practices are critical to the creation of long-term value for all stakeholders. This chapter describes how these two factories address workers' rights, their relationship with buyers, management strategy, and government support to be sustainable in the global market. The findings demonstrate that they have chosen a high-road strategy, believing that if employees are treated well by their employer, the employees will act in a way that is beneficial for the company. What type of government support the suppliers receive and what expectation they have from the policymakers is also the focus of this chapter.

Chapter 6 critically analyzes managements' perceptions of the transnational governance approaches. The Rana Plaza tragedy triggered the emergence of two significant transnational governance initiatives – the Accord on Fire and Building Safety, and the Alliance for Bangladesh Worker Safety. For the first time, different key stakeholders worked together to address the fire, electrical, and structural safety of factory buildings. After analyzing managements' perception of the Accord and Alliance, this chapter argues that, although there have been significant breakthroughs in terms of developing a culture of safety adhered to by the government and entrepreneurs, the suppliers have encountered difficulties in implementing these initiatives. The limited support from buyers has posed a major challenge for the sustainability of this governance mechanism addressing compliance.

Chapter 7 examines managements' experiences with challenges of sustainability in the global supply chain. These challenges include labour productivity, audit, codes of conduct, ethical price, and upgrading of initiatives. The impact of the COVID-19 on the suppliers, workers, and industry is also analyzed in this chapter, opening up a completely new dimension of sustainability and questions about the role of buyers in the pandemic. Some challenges of sustainability are explored in this chapter, including lack of skilled workforce leading to lower labour productivity, absence of a unified audit system, and constant pressures from buyers to offer low prices to suppliers. To minimize these pressures, factories are being upgraded, but there is also a concern about their sustainability. The last chapter illustrates the ways to address the challenges of the factory management which are presented in different chapters of the book. This indication will ensure the sustainability of the Bangladesh RMG industry.

Acknowledgements

This book has presented the management perception of Bangladesh's export-oriented garment industry in the global supply chain, which would not have been possible without the participation of senior factory management in interviews with me in two research projects. I wish to thank the participants for their time, effort, and enthusiasm. I gratefully acknowledge funding by the Volkswagen Foundation for the project "Changes in the Governance of Garment Global Production Networks: Lead Firm, Supplier, and Institutional Responses to the Rana Plaza Disaster" under the European and Global Challenges Program. I also express my gratitude to Laudes Foundation for funding the project "Scale Matters: Scalability of Business Case Sustainability Initiatives in the Garment Industry." Many thanks to both the project team members as well. I am indebted to the research assistants during fieldwork and editing, particularly Asmaul Anika and Tanjima. Special thanks go to Dorothea Schaefter and Alexandra de Brauw of Routledge, and Rajamalar who spent considerable time and effort providing me with important comments and suggestions. I owe a debt of gratitude to my friend Miru for getting me access to the key stakeholders and our conversations on the garment industry. Finally, I am indebted to my family members, without whom this publication would not have been accomplished.

Glossary

ADB	Asian Development Bank
BB	Back-to-Back
BDHS	Bangladesh Demographic and Health Survey
BGMEA	Bangladesh Garment Manufacturers and Exporters Association
BGSS	Bangladesh Garment Shramik Sanghati
BIGD	Bangladesh Institute of Governance and Development
BKMEA	Bangladesh Knitwear Manufacturers and Exporters Association
BNBC	Bangladesh National Building Code
BOI	Board of Investment
BSCI	Business Social Compliance Initiative
BUET	Bangladesh University of Engineering and Technology
BUFT	BGMEA University of Fashion and Technology
BUTEX	Bangladesh University of Textiles
CAP	Corrective Action Plan
CED	Centre for Entrepreneurship and Development
CPD	Centre for Policy Dialogue
CSR	Corporate Social Responsibility
DEA	Detailed Engineering Assessment
DFI	Development Finance Institution
DIFE	Department of Inspection for Factories and Establishments
EBA	Everything But Arms
ED	Executive Director
EIU	Economist Intelligence Unit
EPB	Export Promotion Bureau
EPIDC	East Pakistan industrial Development Corporation
EPZ	Export Processing Zone
ETP	Effluent Treatment Plan
EU	European Union
FBCCI	Federation of Bangladesh Chamber of Commerce and Industries
GATT	General Agreement of Tariff and Trade
GDP	Gross Domestic Production
GEAR	Gender Equality and Returns
GM	General Manager

GNI	Gross National Income
GSP	Generalized Scheme of Preferences
HR	Human Resources
ICB	Investment Corporation of Bangladesh
IFC	International Finance Corporation
ILO	International Labour Organization
IMF	International Monetary Fund
KII	Key Informant Interviews
LC	Letters of Credit
LDC	Least Developed Country
LR	Lean Retaining
MD	Managing Director
MFA	Multi-Fibre Arrangement
MFN	Most Favoured Nation
MiB	Mapped in Bangladesh
MNC	Multinational Corporation
MP	Member of Parliament
MTU	Management Training Unit
NGO	Non-Government Organization
NI	National Initiative
NIC	Newly Industrializing Country
NIP	New Industrial Policy
OSH	Occupational Safety and Health
PaCT	Partner for Cleaner Textile
PPE	Personal Protective Equipment
QR	Quick Response
RCC	Remediation Coordination Cell
RMG	Ready-Made Garment
RSC	RMG Sustainability Council
SAP	Structural Adjustment Programme
SEIP	Skill for Employment Investment Program
SQP	Supplier Qualification Programme
SRHR	Sexual and Reproductive Health and Rights
STWI	Sweden Textile Water Initiative
TA	Time and Action
TIB	Transparency International Bangladesh
TREES	Towards Resource Efficient and Environmental Sustainability
UD	Utilization Declaration
UL	Underwriters Laboratories
WPC	Worker Participation Committee
WRAP	Worldwide Responsible Accredited Production
WTO	World Trade Organization

1 From least developed to lower-middle-income country

In the 1970s, development economists Faaland and Parkinson described Bangladesh as a test case of development, and Henry Kissinger, the U.S. Secretary of State, described Bangladesh as an international basket case. The pessimism was based on several predicaments. High population density and rapid growth were some of the key factors behind pessimism regarding the survival of Bangladesh – 70 million people within a geographic area of 14,400 sq km growing at 3% per year. The country had extremely scarce natural resources. The potential for expanding the land frontier was already exploited. Achievement of food security for the growing population was a challenge, as the technology used for food production was traditional. The breakup from Pakistan could have harmed the economy as the country was dependent on the West Pakistan market for its major exports – jute, textiles, and tea – and the industrial entrepreneurs were mostly from the West. The country was predominantly rural, with only 8% of the population living in urban areas. Being agro-based, the level of per capita income was extremely low. There was little surplus that could be saved and invested to promote growth. The country could not mobilize enough resources to finance developmental activities. The pace of development depended on the mobilization of foreign resources. After independence in 1971, the relationship with the USA was poor. The rudimentary infrastructure, such as roads and bridges, that the country had was largely destroyed during the nine-month war of independence. The entrepreneur class was mostly of Pakistani origin who left the country after separation from Pakistan. A group of indigenous entrepreneurs for promoting industrial growth was missing in the country.

However, the pessimistic predictions have been proved wrong. The 49 years of economic performance proved wrong the doomsday prediction by the eminent scholars of development from the developed countries. The economic progress was slow during the first two decades of development experience. But it has made substantial progress since the early 1990s that surprised many development specialists. Most significant progress has been on socio-economic aspects that surpassed even the progress made in India. Defying overwhelming odds, Bangladesh has graduated from Least Developed to Lower-Middle-Income Country. The GDP growth has increased from 2.14% in 1972–1979 to 8.15% in 2019; the size of the economy has grown from US$35 billion in the mid-90s to US$348 billion in 2020, per capita income rose from US$320 in the 1970s to US$2,064 in 2020, foreign aid dependence declined from 8% of GDP in the 1980s to just about 2% by the end of 2018. The new identity of Bangladesh is a Lower-Middle-Income country.[1] In the international forum, Bangladesh is now considered as a "development model" in the development discourse.

1.1 Background history of the Bangladesh economy

East Bengal – the region that became East Pakistan (1947–1971) and later Bangladesh – was once a prosperous region of South Asia. In the early nineteenth century, this region was well known as a major producer of silks, cotton, and muslin (plain-woven fine white cotton) products that were exported throughout Asia and Europe. The cotton textile industry of East Bengal was at that time among the greatest industries in the world (Ahmad, 1976). This sector became one of the key sources of employment. Muslin was popular in Europe because of its quality and affordability. In 1787, the entire trade of Dhaka district was about US$10 million – of which about half a million represented cloth for export to Europe (Ahmad, 1976). Ahmad notes that the total value of goods manufactured for European markets amounted to about 1 million U.S. dollars in 1807; in 1810 it declined to half a million, and in 1813 it declined further to only a quarter of a million. This means that the number of export earnings declined gradually. In Bangladesh as elsewhere in the British Empire, the colonial power was interested in providing raw materials for its factories, particularly in textiles and jute, and dumping cheap domestically manufactured goods in the East Bengal market (Humphrey, 1990). The British introduced machine-made cloth into the market and East Bengal's native industry collapsed. Kabeer (2000: 55) remarks:

> As the British textile industry merchandised, Britain sought to eliminate competition from Bengal's textiles through an elaborate network of restrictions and prohibitive duties. Duties of up to 70 and 80 per cent had to be placed on Indian goods to protect the nascent British textile industry and, even within India, the sale of Bengal cloth was restricted, so as to favour British products.

In this process, the prosperous weaving industry of East Bengal was destroyed and a large artisan class lost their employment (Humphrey, 1990). Bangladesh was one of the major exporters of textiles, silk, and sugar, but the flow of industrialization was halted during the 200 years of colonial exploitation. Sir Charles Trevelyan of the East India Company wrote in 1840: "Dacca which used to be the Manchester of India has fallen off from a flourishing town to a very poor and small one" (cited in Kabeer, 2000: 56). The British imperial power destroyed the domestic textile industry and transformed the region into one fully dependent on agriculture. Agriculture became the only occupation available to the people of East Bengal. The industrial fame of this region disintegrated as it was pressed into serving the interests of the colonial power.[2]

In the Pakistani period (1947–1971), East Bengal became East Pakistan. This region was exploited under the colonial power and the same conditions persisted. West Pakistan controlled the economic and political power of the region although a majority of the population lived in East Pakistan. As argued by Humphrey, two salient features of this period were these: like Britain, Pakistan pursued a policy emphasizing the pre-eminent role of the private sector in industrial development, and priority was given to West Pakistan's development, with East Pakistan providing raw materials and markets for West Pakistan's products. In other words, in the first post-colonial period of Bangladesh's history, Pakistan reproduced the powerlessness and economic dispossession that had characterized East Bengal's position within the British Empire.

At the time of partition in 1947, both wings of Pakistan were primarily producers of raw materials: the west wing producing raw cotton and the east being the world's largest producer of raw jute (Dutt, Dasgupta and Chatterjee, 1973).[3] A negligible number of industrial establishments were located in East Pakistan. West Pakistan developed its industrial sector ignoring East Pakistan. Over 25 years of Pakistan's history, economic disparity widened between the two regions. Funds were allotted for the West Pakistanis and East Pakistan's resources were drained for the enrichment of the western region. About 56% of the population of Pakistan lived in the eastern wing although the eastern wing accounted for one-seventh of Pakistan's total area (Dutt, Dasgupta and Chatterjee, 1973). According to the popular Pakistani newspaper *The Dawn* (1956), only 51 East Pakistanis were employed in civil service jobs, such as Secretaries, Joint Secretaries, and Deputy Secretaries, etc., while the number of West Pakistanis employed in these jobs was 690. A panel of economic advisers to the Planning Commission of the Government of Pakistan reported that in 1969–1970 the per capita income in West Pakistan was 61% higher than it was in the East (cited in Dutt, Dasgupta and Chatterjee, 1973). The report also found that less than one-fourth of total development expenditure, in both the public and private sector, went to East Pakistan – although East Pakistan's share of Pakistan's total foreign exchange earnings varied between 50% and 70%. From 1948 to 1961 there took place a net transfer of about 180 million rupees from East Pakistan to West Pakistan (cited in Dutt, Dasgupta and Chatterjee, 1973).[4] Funds were allotted for the West Pakistanis, and East Pakistan's resources were depleted for the enrichment of the western region.

By analyzing the social and economic history of Bangladesh from the British to the Pakistan period, we find that its economy was consciously stagnated until the gaining of independence in 1971. The British rulers destroyed the skill of the artisan class and turned the region into an agricultural country. During the Pakistani period, there was extreme disparity concerning the economic development between its two regions.[5]

1.2 From nationalization to trade liberalization policy

Before Independence in Bangladesh in 1971, the industrial enterprises were set up and owned by entrepreneurs, mostly of Pakistani origin. The major industries were jute and cotton textiles, paper and steel mills, tea processing, and paper mills. Some big industries requiring large investments such as fertilizer and steel were set up by the government under the East Pakistan Industrial Development Corporation (EPIDC). The objective was that when mature they would be handed over to the private sector companies. In 1971 there were 3,051 industrial units. About 47% of fixed assets were industries owned by entrepreneurs of Pakistani origin and 18% by private entrepreneurs of Bangladeshi origin. After the war of liberation following Independent Bangladesh in 1971, most of the industrialists of Pakistani origin left Bangladesh. The Bangladesh government took control of the management of those industries and decided to nationalize other big industries owned by Bangladeshi entrepreneurs. The new government implemented a socialist economy that had been promised during the independence struggle (Stepanek, 1979). As a first step, the government nationalized all the key industries including the jute, cotton textile, and sugar industries (Karim, 1996). The West Pakistanis who fled during the war owned the majority of these industrial enterprises. The government of Bangladesh seized their plants as abandoned properties. In addition to the industrial sector, the banking and insurance fields were nationalized. The scope of the private sector was limited to small and cottage industries. As a part of an import-substituting industrialization strategy, quantitative restrictions on imports were extensively employed (Rahman and Bakht, 1996).

The debate about the choice of nationalization lingers on. It can be explained in two ways – political choices or a response to the devastating condition of the economy after the war. It was a political decision of the ruling party to nationalize the key sectors of the economy. This policy originated in the political manifesto of the ruling party. In this context, Sobhan (2005: 7) argues: "This party's political commitment to extend state ownership over the economy dated back to 1954 and was renewed again in 1970 when they won elections to the national and provincial legislatures of Pakistan." The major contribution to the growth of the state-controlled economy originated in the historical circumstances created by the liberation of Bangladesh. The international political climate also played a role in encouraging a socialist approach to national economic development. In other words, it was the political and ideological links between Bangladesh and national liberation or communist movements in other countries.

In addition to ideology, socio-economic conditions also made socialism the only system capable of helping the country to convalesce. At the time of liberation in 1971, business and commercial sectors were dominated by non-Bengalis. The Pakistanis played a discriminatory role toward Bengalis and did not provide opportunities for the Bengalis to take an active part in the private sector. However, after the war, these non-Bengalis withdrew from Bangladesh. Papanek argued that: "This precipitous withdrawal of the Pakistanis left a major entrepreneurial vacuum at the heart of the Bangladesh economy since this non-Bengalis were largely drawn from a few ethnic communities specializing in commerce" (cited in Sobhan, 2005: 6). Bengali entrepreneurs accounted for 18% of manufacturing assets and Bengali-owned banks accounted for 18% of deposits (Sobhan and Ahmad, 1980). There were 725 enterprises in Bangladesh when the non-Bengalis business class left Bangladesh (Sobhan, 2005). As Bangladesh had not developed a domestic class of entrepreneurs and no efficient management system existed, the government had to grapple with the abandoned enterprises.

However, there was a lot of confusion about the control of the nationalized enterprises (Humphrey, 1990). As part of the nationalization policy, the government established several sectoral corporations to ensure the coordination of government control, such as the Bangladesh Jute Industries Corporation, an industry that included 77 enterprises. According to the Planning Commission, even though it was the responsibility of the corporation to manage enterprises under each corporation, ministers often chose to demonstrate power over the corporations. As a result, the management problem was acute in terms of running these nationalized enterprises. Due to the lack of a Bengali capitalist class, there were no qualified personnel to play the role of managers. Party workers of the government were found to fill the gap (Karim, 1996). Incompetent, inexperienced, and unqualified personnel ran the public enterprises. As a result, mismanagement, pilferage, and corruption became rampant. The prices of goods and services were set by the government which did not reflect actual market conditions. As a result, public enterprises produced high-priced but not quality products. The production was also low due to a lack of incentives and inadequate entrepreneurial knowledge. Furthermore, because of low production and declining revenues, state enterprises were incurring huge losses. It became evident that the country's economy was not growing. Manufacturing made up 7.3% of GDP in 1972 but only 7.4% by 1975 (Humphrey, 1990). All these factors contributed to the failure of nationalization.

The nationalization of the economy ended in Bangladesh when a new government took control in 1975. The new government focussed on the need to boost Bangladeshi production – especially in food and grains – and to integrate rural development through a variety of programmes. The ideology of this government was market-oriented, and its goal was to achieve higher growth through the development of the private sector by privatization. It believed that widening the private sector – rather than the public sector – would stimulate economic growth. But the government did not privatize all sectors at once; rather, it gradually opened the economy. Humphrey (1990) notes that sectors, including paper, iron and steel, and oil and gas, were immediately opened to private ownership. Potential export sectors such as jute and textiles were reserved for public ownership. To inspire investment in industry, a special bank was established – the Bangladesh Shilpa Bank. The Investment Corporation of Bangladesh was authorized and the Dhaka Stock Exchange was reactivated. These market-friendly policies encouraged Bengali business people in terms of longer-term industrial investment. Between 1973–1974 and 1980–1981, industrial production increased by 45%: the private sector grew by 64% while the public sector grew by 39%. Humphrey also claims that despite the development of the private sector, raw jute and jute manufacturers – which remained part of the public sector – earned 75% of the foreign exchange. The ground was well prepared for the next step in the evolution of a privatization policy (Humphrey, 1990; Quadir, 2000).

While the policy reforms introduced by the previous governments had reduced the role of government in the allocation of resources and production, the government in the 1980s directly controlled all private industrial investment as well as the allocation of domestic credit and foreign exchange (Mallon and Stern, 1991). The New Industrial Policy was declared in June 1982. Karim (1996) has analyzed some of the features of this policy. Decentralization of jute and cotton textile mills and decentralization of investment approval and loan disbursement procedures were prominent among the new policies. This is reflected in larger investment allocation – over 35% of the investment budget for the private sector during 1980–1985 compared to 11% in the 1970s (1973–1978) (Karim, 1996). The Foreign Private Investment Promotion Act was introduced to promote foreign private investment. Private banks and insurance companies were also introduced. Private investment increased fourfold between 1980 and 1985 (Karim, 1996). The government established an export-processing zone (EPZ) in Chittagong in 1983. Joint ventures, 100% foreign-owned investments, and 100% Bangladeshi-owned companies were all permitted to operate and enjoy equal treatment

Table 1.1 Changes in GDP growth (in percentages)

Indicators	*1973–1979*[a]	*1980–1990*[a]	*1992–1998*[b]	*2010*	*2019*
GDP growth rate	2.14	4.36	5.4	5.57	8.15

a Sattar (1997).
b Rahman and Bhattacharya (2000) and BBS (2019).

Table 1.2 Share of major sectors to GDP, 1972–2019 (in percentages)

Sectors	*1972*	*1980*	*1997*	*2009*	*2019*
Agriculture	49.5	40.9	30.0	17.1	12.68
Industry	7.9	10.8	11.8	25.3	29.65
Services	42.6	48.3	58.2	53.32	52.85

Sources: Rahman and Bhattacharya (2000) and BBS (2019).

in the EPZs. The pace of reforms in the 1980s was significantly influenced by the Structural Adjustment Programmes (SAPs) of the World Bank and the International Monetary Fund (Dijkstra, 2002; Haque, 2002; Rahman and Bakht, 1996; Stiglitz, 1999). To promote industrial growth the government introduced wide-ranging reforms through the Industrial Policy of 1991. Important provisions were as follows:

- Industrialization followed a process of liberalization and deregulation.
- The government's role in the industrial process became supportive instead of regulatory.
- The government created a favourable environment for foreign investment in setting up the industrial establishment.
- The list of discouraged industries introduced earlier was dropped.
- Nationalized banks and development finance institutions (DFIs) to sanction projects up to Tk. 30 crores as against the previous ceiling of Tk. 10 crores.
- Export-oriented industries became exempted from payment of any taxes.
- The limit of equity participation for foreign enterprises had been raised from 51% to 100%.
- The expansion of small and cottage industries was promoted for the generation of employment.

The economic policies pursued during the 1990s were aimed at alleviating poverty through growth, economic liberalization, privatization of state-owned enterprises, incentives for private investment, and reform of the banking system. Efforts to achieve Bangladesh's macroeconomic goals, however, have been problematic. The privatization of public sector industries has proceeded at a slow pace, due in part to worker unrest in the affected industries. In the 1990s, only 12 state-owned enterprises were privatized during 1991–1996 and four during 1996–2000 (The Economist Intelligence Unit [EIU], 1999). During 1991–1996, the government emphasized market-based policies to stimulate the growth rate. Rapid liberalization of the economy continued during the 1990s. According to the EIU (1999), the overall economy grew at an annual rate of 5% in the 1990s compared to 4% in the 1980s. The top customs duty rate was cut from 350% in 1991 to 37.5% by 1999.

The government concentrated on export growth, the gradual lowering of tariffs and import controls to achieve rapid industrialization. The liberalization of industrial policies in the 1990s has reduced bureaucratic control over private investment. The Board of Investment was given the task of facilitating investments, import controls were reduced, and import permits were abolished (EIU, 1999). Firms located in EPZs can import capital and raw materials free of import duty, retain foreign currency earnings, employ expatriates and non-unionized labour, and enjoy a ten-year tax holiday. In terms of investment, employment, and exports, the country's two EPZs have been extremely successful. According to the Bureau of Economic and Business Affairs (2000), the 143 companies operating in the EPZs represent a cumulative investment of over US$400 million, employ 92,000 people, and generate about US$700 million in export earnings each year.

The government declared another industrial policy in 2010 as part of the implementation of the 2010–2021 Perspective Plan: The key objective of industrialization was the reduction of poverty. Priority is given to the establishment of medium and small-scale industries with labour-intensive rather than capital-intensive production processes. Special incentives continue to be provided to promote faster development of export-oriented industries. Encouragement is also given to set up import-substituting industries wherever possible. The government has provided a supervisory role to promote dynamism and efficiency of the private sector, rather than been directly involved in industrial production. Due to the adoption of trade liberalization policy during different periods and the current industrial policy, the GDP growth rate increased from 2.14% in the 1970s to 5.4% in the 1990s and reached 8.15% in 2019 (see Table 1.1). The service sector dominates the share of GDP in the country's economy. The GDP share of agriculture declined from 49.5% in 1972 to 12.68% in 2019, while the share of industry increased to 29.65% in the same period (see Table 1.2).

1.3 Five pillars of development

After independence, a major obstacle for development was higher population growth. People thought children, particularly boys are assets, as they can be used to work as domestic helpers in farming before they form their own family. They could also look after the parents at old age. Experience however showed that if the children are poor, they would not help the parents at old age. With the decline in the importance of farming and the availability of modern amenities for life, the number of children was considered a hindrance to a better life. With the availability of means for population planning and the government's aggressive campaign for population control, the fertility rate started declining. The fertility rate has been reduced from over 6% in the early 1980s to 2.3% in 2014. The birth rate has declined much faster than the death rate. The population growth rate has declined from 2.5% per year in the 1970s to 1.1% now. The advantages of slow population growth are several. The proportion of children 0–15 years of age has declined from 45% to 32% over the last two decades. The proportion of the working-age population has increased by over 10%. As a result, the dependency ratio has declined substantially. The household has to spend less on basic needs, such as food, education, and healthcare. It generated the capacity to save and invest that drives the growth of income. The government has less need to invest in research, irrigation, and input subsidies to produce more food. There is less compulsion to develop social infrastructures, such as schools and hospitals. The savings could be invested in the development of physical infrastructures, such as roads, bridges, port facilities, and power supply, which remain in short supply. The crude death rate has also declined from 12.1 per 1,000 in 1985 to 5.5 in 2011. Most of the reduction is due to a drastic decline in the rate of mortality of under-five children. The under-five mortality has declined from 150 per 10,000 women in the 1970s to 47 in 2014, and the infant mortality from 132 in 1980 to only 38 in 2014. This data show that Bangladesh has made good progress in terms of population control, which has a significant impact on the development of the country.

Self-sufficiency in rice production is another area of achievement in Bangladesh. The area under cultivated land has been declining due to demand for land for habitation, industrialization, commercialization, and infrastructure development. Despite the decline, rice production has increased from 17.6 million metric tonnes in 1975–1976 to 34.5 million metric tonnes in 2013–2014, with export of 12,500 metric tonnes to Sri Lanka in 2015 (Misra, 2019). As a result, the rate of hunger has reduced drastically. The progress made in food grain production was mostly due to the development of improved technologies (high yielding varieties) by the research system, and their adoption by small, marginal, and mostly illiterate farmers. The adoption was facilitated by the rapid investment by farmers on shallow tube wells and power pumps. The irrigated area has now increased to 80% of cultivated land, and the adoption of improved varieties has reached almost 90%. The government also supported it by the expansion of credit and provision of input subsidies to support self-sufficiency in food grain production. To ensure food security, the government spends 2% of GDP on different safety-net programmes, such as vulnerable group feeding, vulnerable group development, provision of food for workers, old age pensions, and support for destitute women.

The development of rural roads and the expansion of micro-credit for the poor are also the factors behind the transformation of the economy of Bangladesh (Table 1.3). The government made heavy investments in rural roads, connecting villages with local markets and Upazila headquarters with paved roads. The roads generated employment for agricultural workers in rural transport and trading operations. The generation of agricultural surplus due to the rapid expansion of agricultural technology and demand

Table 1.3 Impact of five pillars of development

Sectors	*Achievements*
Population growth	1979: 2.7%; 2018: 1.1%
Rice production	1975–1976: 17.6; 2013–2014: 34.5 (million metric tons)
Remittance	1981: $350 million; 2019: $18.32 billion
RMG export earning	1978: $10,000; 2016:$28.67 billion
Microfinance	2020: 629 NGOs have mobilized about 13.85 million poor people. 11.85 million are female, disbursed BDT 164.26 billion

Source: BBS (2015), World Bank (2018), Bangladesh Bank (2019) and Misra (2019).

for food from a rapidly growing urban population created a demand for services in trade and agro-business. The small-scale petty trading was supported by the rapid expansion of the micro-credit programme of Grameen Bank. A socio-economic study of credit operation in a village near Chittagong University (Zobra) by Professor M. Yunus laid the foundation of the micro-credit model in 1976. The study observed that many low-income households operate tiny economic activities by taking loans from moneylenders with a very high rate of interest, often 10% per month. After paying the interest and the principal, the borrower has very little surplus left to accumulate savings to expand the business. The operators are thus perpetually dependent on moneylenders for high-interest loans that sustains the vicious circle of poverty. If credit could be extended to these households on easy terms, they could save small amounts at the end of each loan cycle, increase equity in the business, and move on a ladder for poverty reduction. But banks do not consider them credit-worthy since the size of the loan they demand is tiny, and they cannot offer any collateral that could be invoked in case of default. Dr Yunus went to a nearby branch of a Krishi Bank and pleaded to give them loans under his guarantee. Since the borrowers are engaged in activities that generate regular incomes (cottage industries, petty trade, etc.), he developed a weekly loan repayment system that suits the circumstances of low-income households. The loans were all repaid in time to the surprise of the bank officials. The Grameen model was offered to households through women members, as they are found more responsible with money, and giving control over money could help to empower women. The Grameen Bank model was accepted by many NGOs in Bangladesh engaged in empowering the poor through community development. Grameen Bank, ASA, and BRAC alone extends credit to nearly 18 million households. The NGOs mainly through micro-credit programmes have paved the path of rural development as well as women empowerment in the country.

The generation of employment for unskilled workers in the overseas markets is another reason for the development of Bangladesh. Remittance from this migrated workforce is a key source of foreign currency for the country. The ageing of the population in developed counties and fast economic growth in middle-income countries has created a demand for unskilled labour in low-paid jobs such as construction labour and manual services. Bangladesh was able to take advantage of the demand and could send low-educated unemployed workers abroad. During the 1950s and 1960s, the migration trend was towards Western countries, but this pattern changed dramatically during the 1970s due to the oil boom in the Arabian Gulf. In response to the high demand for Bangladeshi workers in Middle Eastern countries, created by the oil price hike and major infrastructure development projects, the supply of labour from Bangladesh to the international market grew substantially after the country established independence from Pakistan in 1971 (Siddiqui, 2003). In 2008, Bangladesh exported nearly 900,000 workers abroad. The export has declined since then, but still, about 0.5 million workers leave for overseas jobs, which accounts for about one-third of the new entrants in the labour force. Overseas migration has eased the pressure on the government of finding jobs for the new entrants to the labour force within the country. Now, a third of the new entrants to the labour force finds employment overseas. The foreign exchange component of the remittance fuels the wheels of the economy by supplying much-needed foreign exchange for financing essential imports for development. The remittance from overseas migrants had a steep upward trend over the last decade reaching almost $14 billion in 2012, about 11% of the gross national income, second to export earnings from RMGs. The remittance helps to improve the living standards of the relatives left behind by the migrants. It is an important source of finance for setting up trade and business, improvement in housing, and accumulation of land. It has also helped finance imports of raw materials and machinery for infrastructure development and helped expand the home market for industries.

The development of labour-intensive export-oriented industries is the crucial factor behind the rapid transformation of the economy of Bangladesh. Since independence, the Bangladeshi economy has been dependent on agriculture, and most of the population has been living in rural areas. But since the 1980s the development of the export sector has come to be seen as increasingly important. After the collapse of the jute regime, the government's attention turned towards the manufacturing sector, especially the garment industry, as the new engine for economic growth. The 1980s mark the beginning of the rapid integration of Bangladesh's small and often home-based garment industry into the global garment chain. In the 1970s and 1980s, the nation depended so heavily on foreign aid that the international community speculated that there was no possibility of the country developing without aid and that dependency on aid would therefore continue. But the emergence of the garment industry has challenged that idea. Bangladesh is now able to reduce its dependence on aid; rather the country searches for a favourable trade agreement. A significant change occurred in the 1980s in the structure of the export sector. The combination of jute, cotton, textiles, paper, and tobacco – which had represented 60% of production in 1974 – dropped to 40% by 1985, while growth was greater in garment exports (Humphrey, 1990). As a result, industrial growth – which was 3.7% in 1983 – reached 9% in 1984–1985 (Humphrey, 1990). The garment industry now accounts for three-fourths of our export earnings, and generate employment for over 4 million workers. Impressive growth in the export-oriented garment industry continues to strengthen industrial growth in the country. Many new jobs – mostly for women – have been created by the country's dynamic private RMG industry.

As a result of these factors, Bangladesh reduced poverty from 44.2% in 1991 to 14.8% in 2016–2017 based on a poverty line of $1.90 per day. In addition to the above-mentioned five pillars of development, there are other areas in the country that have achieved immense progress. Electricity is a major source of energy in the industrial and agricultural sectors of development. The electricity sector in Bangladesh has one national grid with an installed capacity of 21,419 MW as of September 2019. In 1992 only 12% of the population had access to electricity and now it has increased to 95% of the population. Urbanization is also an inevitable process of development. Almost 60% of the growth of the population of Dhaka city has been due to rural to urban migration. Because of the concentration of services and demand for goods, the return on education and capital is much higher in urban than in rural areas. Urbanization promotes occupational mobility from low-paying jobs (such as agricultural labour) to high-paying jobs (such as industrial labour, construction labour, driving, and retail trade), even with the same level of education and skills. It also promotes social and cultural development through higher literacy rates, improves the quality of education, helps to provide better healthcare, and results in the cultivation of traditional and modern culture through different forms of arts.

However, Bangladesh has made a greater achievement in social development. When Amartya Sen was asked why India couldn't do several things that Bangladesh had done, Sen said:

> Why has Bangladesh been able to do so many things that we have not been able to. The spread of education among girls in Bangladesh is far higher than both in Bengal and India. They (girls in Bangladesh) have more access to health care. Their life expectancy is higher than in girls in India. It is also true that they (in Bangladesh) have more educational opportunities in school. Why do these differences exist? We are both Bengali (people). We need to think about this.
>
> (The Telegraph, 2020)

The Nobel laureate argued that initiatives by NGOs such as BRAC, Grameen Bank, and Gonoshasthaya Kendra contributed significantly to the country's progress, as did the government's well-thought-out action plan aiming at the empowerment of women in Bangladesh. The emergence of the RMG showcases the contribution of women to transform the country from LDC to a Lower-Middle-Income Country.

Notes

1 Since the country has entered the GNI per capita range between $1,046 and $4,125 per year to gain the status, Bangladesh is considered as a Lower-Middle-Income country.
2 This is the process that has been explained by Frank (1967), Baran (1957), Sweezy (1968) and Wallerstein (1987) in analyzing the reasons for underdevelopment in the Third World.
3 The British divided the subcontinent into India and Pakistan and it marked independence for both states, while the Bangladesh region became known as East Pakistan.
4 Rupee is Pakistan's currency as well as India's. During the period of 1950–1970, one U.S. dollar was equal to about ten rupees.
5 Both regimes fit the dependency view that the developing countries had a history of exploitation and the adverse effects on their economies resulted from dominant and powerful external forces. Frank (1967), Baran (1957), Sweezy (1968) and Wallerstein (1987) have explained this process in their dependency theories.

2 From million to billion-dollar industry

During the colonial period, the jute industry had played an important role in the economic development of Bengal, of which modern Bangladesh was part. Raw jute was mainly produced in East Bengal as conditions were favourable for the cultivation of jute. Before the establishment of jute mills, handloom weavers used jute fibre to make twines, ropes, and coarse fabrics for the poor, and also for other purposes. Towards the end of the eighteenth century, jute drew the attention of the British colonizers and it was later exported to other countries.[1] After the Partition of India in 1947 all jute mills of the region fell in West Bengal, which became a part of India and all major jute-growing districts became part of East Pakistan (which later became Bangladesh). Without a mill, East Pakistan faced problems in marketing its raw jute. The problem was, however, quickly overcome by establishing jute mills in East Pakistan. After independence in 1971, raw jute became the only major export item of Bangladesh, as 70 jute mills were established during the Pakistan period. The jute industry produced about 600,000 tonnes of jute goods in 1969–1970 and employed 200,000 workers. Internal consumption was 250,000 tonnes and 65,000 tonnes were exported to West Pakistan and other countries (Ahmad, 1976). In the world export of raw jute, Bangladesh's share was 61% in 1970–1971 and in the world export of manufactured jute, the share was 45.5% in 1970. After a virtual monopoly of over a century, the jute industry declined in importance after 1970. During the 1970s, the industry confronted hard competition from synthetic substitutes commonly known as polypropylene. Polypropylene is preferred as a packing material since it is much cheaper, easy to manufacture, highly durable, and lightweight. After losing the market to polypropylene, many jute mills in Western countries were closed down and the jute industry of the subcontinent experienced troubling times. In 1980–1981, the proportion of jute and jute goods in the export sector was 68.21%. Within ten years, this dropped to 26.91%. After the collapse of the jute regime, the government's attention turned to the role of the export-oriented garment industry, as the new engine for economic growth. The 1980s marked the beginning of the rapid integration of Bangladesh's ready-made garment (RMG) industry into the global garment chain.

2.1 Origin of the Bangladesh RMG

In 1980–1981 the proportion of garments in the export sector of Bangladesh was only 0.42%, but at the beginning of the new millennium, its share of exports reached 75.66%, thereby making it the major contributor to Bangladeshi exports (Board of Investment Bangladesh, 2002). One of the reasons for this success was the introduction of a global trade agreement, known as the Multi-fibre Arrangement (MFA). The MFA was an international agreement, signed and negotiated by the governments of 44 countries in 1974 (the number of member countries increased later) to provide for special rules governing trade in textiles and the clothing industry. "The MFA contained a series of bilaterally negotiated quota restrictions covering trade in both textiles and clothing between individual developed and developing countries" (Trela and Whalley, 1990: 13). Under the quota, the exporter was allowed to supply a certain volume of textile and clothing products, and the amount of quota was negotiated between the importing and exporting countries (Smith, 2003). The MFA provided the basis on which industrialized countries had been able to restrict imports from developing nations especially "Asian Tigers." Import-competing firms in the developed countries justifiably feared that the rapid growth of imports from the cost-competitive developing world would threaten their jobs and the viability of their textile and clothing industry (Smith, 2003). Consequently, the developed world had placed increasingly restrictive protectionist measures against the import of textile and apparel from developing countries under the auspices of the MFA, a strategy which was a violation of the principles of the General Agreement of Tariff and Trade (GATT).[2]

The industrialized nations were the main initiators of this kind of agreement and they imposed it to protect their domestic industries and to support a large number of local employees in this sector. Gerard et al. (1981: 9) argues that the reason for the development of this complex system of protection was that

> There is no alternative employment for a large section of the labour force employed in these industries in industrialized countries, especially because the industry is concentrated in declining regions and employs disadvantaged segments of the population, above all women and minorities.

Appelbaum (2004) also supports the view that the quotas protected jobs in industrial countries. Appelbaum interprets the IMF-World Bank estimates the following way: protecting a single job in the industrial core causes 35 jobs to be lost in developing countries under the MFA.

The MFA had a very different impact on countries, depending on whether they were classified as Least Developed Countries (LDCs) or not. MFA restrictions negatively affected the non-LDC countries such as Hong Kong, Taiwan, and the Republic of Korea, who are the main exporters of textiles and clothing. For example, in 1981, 73% of Korean exports of such goods were subject to MFA quotas, and by 1987 this had risen to 97% (Smith, 2003). A high quota utilization rate indicates that the quotas were restraining the volume that suppliers were able to export. In this way, MFA quotas had been cited as an obstacle for the Korean textile and clothing producers as well as for other advanced developing countries. On the other hand, the MFA worked as a catalyst for most of the LDCs. Since the European Union (EU) did not impose quotas on LDCs, Bangladesh acquired an advantage over non-LDCs such as Korea and Hong Kong (CAFOD, 1998). Until 1985, Bangladesh operated as a quota-free territory, a factor that greatly facilitated the early growth of the garment industry. In subsequent years the United Kingdom, France, Canada, and the U.S. imposed quotas on the import of Bangladeshi garments as per the MFA (Rock, 2001). In the first half of 1986, a high-level delegation of the Bangladesh Garment Manufacturer and Exporter Association (BGMEA) went to Washington DC and Brussels to negotiate the deal. As a result, the U.K. and the French quotas were largely withdrawn and the U.S. quotas were relaxed. The policymakers of Bangladesh strongly believe that if they did not get favourable treatment as a result of the MFA they might not be able to integrate activities into the global market and develop their manufacturing capabilities (Siddiqi, 2004). The introduction of the MFA is thereby considered the key factor behind the rapid development of the Bangladesh garment industry.

Box 2.1 Timeline of the Bangladesh RMG

1978: RMG industry started its journey with $10,000 exports made by 1,200 workers
1985: Export reached $116 million, 0.12 million workers, and 384 factories
1995: Export hit $2.2 billion, eliminated Child Labour through Earn Learn programme
2005: Export $6.4 billion, quota phased out which was predicted to have severe adverse effects
2010: Export $12.5 billion, Ranked second-largest RMG exporting country despite global recession
2013: Export $21.52 billion, Accord and Alliance launched in response to Rana Plaza
2016: Export hit $28.67 billion, Major progress in safety workers' rights
2020: RMG Sustainability Council replaced Accord-Alliance, COVID-19 devastated the sector

Source: BGMEA (2020).

Since the quotas under the MFA were bilateral, buyers and producers had been keen to move operations to the quota-free regions of the world. Despite modern technology and rich infrastructure, even companies in more advanced developing countries fell victim to the MFA regime. They were consequently eager to relocate their production to the quota-free countries – particularly to the poorest of the LDCs even though infrastructure there was very rudimentary. As a result, the established garment exporters of Newly Industrialized Countries (NICs) such as South Korea, Hong Kong, and Taiwan moved operations to Bangladesh and other LDCs. Quddus and Rashid further state that if the LDCs had to depend solely on market forces, the rapid development of the garment industry in these countries might have been delayed by years. According to the American Textile Manufacturers Institute (cited in Appelbaum, 2004: 6): "Dozens of countries which currently ship textiles and apparel to the United States would not be doing so if initially Japan, then Hong Kong, Taiwan, South Korea and, finally, China, were not subject to control." The process started in the late 1970s when the Asian Tiger countries were looking for ways to circumvent the export quotas of Western countries. In their search, they discovered Bangladesh as a potential investment region (Custers, 1997). A significant example of the impact of this behaviour by the Asian Tigers on industrialization in LDCs was the collaboration of the domestic private garment firm in Bangladesh, the Desh Company, with a Korean company, Daewoo in 1978. Daewoo, a major exporter of garments, was looking for opportunities in countries that had barely used their quotas since the quota limitations imposed on Korea under the MFA were restricting Daewoo's exports. As an LDC, Bangladesh had the opportunity to export garments without any restrictions, and for this reason Daewoo became interested in establishing operations in Bangladesh. As part of its global strategies, the Daewoo Corporation of South Korea became interested in Bangladesh when the Chairman, Kim Woo-Choong, proposed an ambitious joint venture to the government of Bangladesh which involved the development and operation of the tyre, leather goods, cement, and garment factories (Rock, 2001). According to Bhattacharya and Rahman (2001), the Desh-Daewoo collaboration was crucial in terms of accessing the global apparel markets at a crucial juncture, when importing restructuring was taking place in this market after the signing of the MFA in 1974. Daewoo, a major exporter of garments, was looking for opportunities in countries that were not utilizing their full quota. Due to the quota limitation for Korea after MFA, Daewoo's export quota was restricted. Due to Bangladesh's advantage of exporting without restriction, Daewoo showed immense interest to invest in the RMG industry of Bangladesh. Behind this logic was the development of a relationship of mutual but unequal dependence: Bangladesh came to depend on Daewoo for imported raw materials, while Daewoo gained access to markets in developed countries. When the Chairman of Daewoo showed interest in Bangladesh, the country's President put him in touch with the chairman of Desh Company, who was looking to expand his entrepreneurial activities (Mahmood, 2002).

Daewoo signed a five-year collaboration agreement with Desh Company in 1980 which included collaborations in the areas of technical training, purchase of machinery and fabric, plant set-up, and marketing, in return for a specific marketing commission on all exports by Desh during the contract period (Rock, 2001). Daewoo also provided in-depth practical training to Desh employees in the working environment of a multinational company. Daewoo actively collaborated with Desh in purchasing machinery and fabrics. Some Daewoo technicians came to Bangladesh to set up the plant for Desh. The outcome of the collaboration was significant. In the first six years of its operation, i.e. 1980/1981–1986/1987, Desh's export value grew at an annual average rate of 90%, reaching more than $5 million in 1986/1987 (Mahmood, 2002).

The Desh-Daewoo partnership was an important factor in the expansion and success of Bangladesh's entire garments export sector. In the first place, by being associated with Daewoo's brand names and marketing network, Bangladesh received world apparel market exposure. Foreign buyers identified it as a positive sourcing place. Second, as Mahmood (2002) explains, many trainees left Desh Company at various times to set up their competing garment firms. As a result, the training these employees received from Daewoo spread throughout the country. Another important factor is that Desh-Daewoo collaboration influenced government policy. Previously, it was a very difficult job for business people to gain approval for joint ventures from the government. But the owner of Desh Company was able to break this pattern because he was a senior in the bureaucracy. The President of Bangladesh, Ziaur Rahman, at that time, also showed interest in the implementation of the Desh-Daewoo collaboration. When the government found that the partnership was a rapid success, the government began to formulate a broader domestic policy for the garment industry.

Another reason for the recent growth of the Bangladesh garment industry is the trade-friendly policy initiated by the government. One of the important measures that the Bangladeshi government has introduced for the garment industry is Back-to-Back Letters of Credit (BB/LC).[3] This scheme has helped the Bangladesh garment industry in two ways. First, the Bangladeshi garment owners do not need the capital to import goods because the buyer or supplier arranges the materials for the exporter through the banks. Second, as banks make profits through the LC system, positive relations between banks and garment entrepreneurs have been strengthened. Another major government initiative is the inception of bonded warehouse facilities in 1980. Under this policy, garment-related accessories can be imported free of duty as the garment industry is a 100% export-oriented industry. After importing the inputs, the entrepreneurs keep the materials in a store of the factory and the customs officers inspect the materials. A condition of the bonded warehouse facility is that all imported materials must be used for the garment industry. If any entrepreneurs sell these imported resources to the domestic market, they are subject to governmental penalties. Before this policy's inception, there was a high duty on the import of garment-related materials. The cost of production was higher and the net profit was thereby lower. But the implementation of this policy has favoured the garment industry and it can offer consumers its products at a lower price. Under the cash compensation scheme, domestic suppliers to export-oriented RMG factories used to receive a cash payment equivalent to 10% of the value addition of the exported RMG. Under the export-led development strategy, the government of Bangladesh has undertaken other steps to compete in the world trade market. Tariff reforms have become a high priority in the government's policy reforms. Average tariff rates have been significantly reduced. The average tariff on all products was reduced from 114% in 1989 to 22% in 1999 (Mujeri and Khondker, 2002). The government has also ensured clarity, simplicity, and transparency in tariff administration.

2.2 The structure of the Bangladesh garment industry

From the above discussion of the background history of the garment industry, it is evident that the favourable treatment under the MFA, government policy, and the Desh-Daewoo collaboration have played crucial roles in developing this industry. According to the data, more than 3,500 factories are now operating. These factories are mainly located in Dhaka, Gazipur, Narayangonj, Ashulia, Savar, Chittagong, and some in Export Processing Zones (EPZ). In 2018, the export earning was $32.92 billion and the target for 2021 is $50 billion. The RMG industry has become a billion-dollar industry within two decades. The sector has provided job opportunities for more than 4 million workers, whose lives are now deeply linked with the success or failure of this industry (Figure 2.1).

The journey of the RMG sector started with only 384 factories in the year 1984 (BGMEA, 2020). By 1992–1993, the number of garment factories was 1,537; within seven years, this figure doubled (see Table 2.1). According to the data, more than 4,500 factories are now operating. As of present, the total number of current active garments factories stands out to be a debatable figure with different sources reporting different numbers. This is mostly attributed to inadequate information on factories before the Rana Plaza incident, the tragedy which cost more than a thousand lives and called for safety compliances in these factories, and as such, they need to record the total number of factories that became relevant. Since most data rely on the BGMEA data list, there are no unified reports which consolidate and conclude a proper figure of the total active factories. This is perhaps best illustrated by the "drop" in the number of factories listed on the BGMEA website after the Rana Plaza incident, from 5,876 factories in 2012–2013 to the currently 4,621. The BGMEA felt that it would be rational to omit these factories from the record due to the inability to locate them; otherwise, they would be liable if the factories had an accident. A massive effort is now in operation to find out the total number of export-oriented garment factories in Bangladesh.[4] Another problematic area of the structure of the

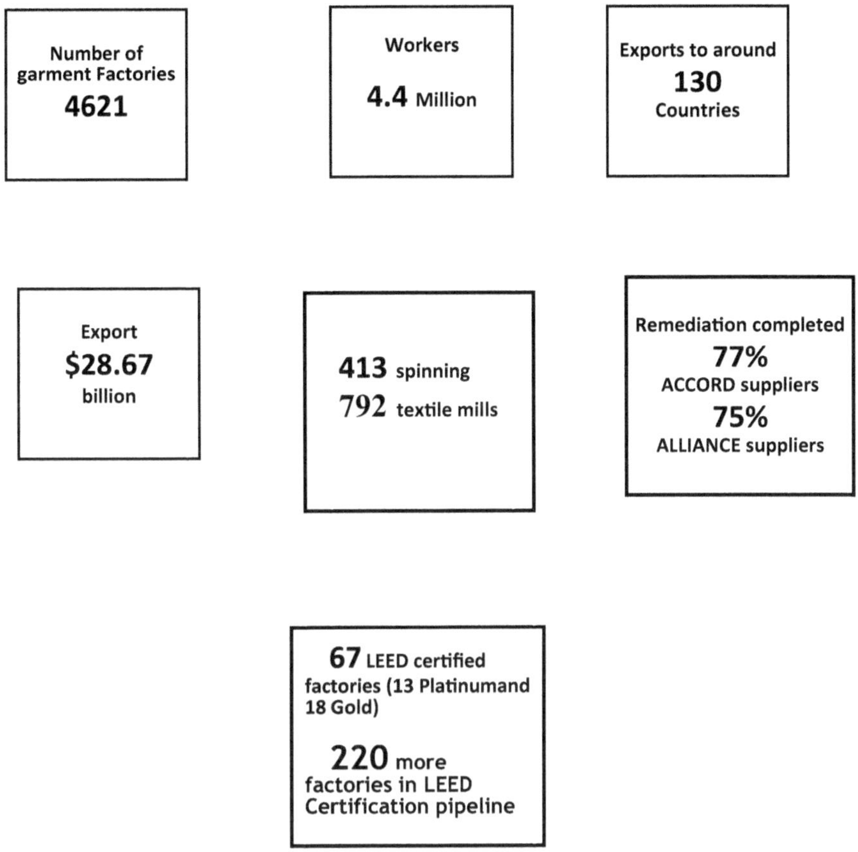

Figure 2.1 Snapshot of Bangladesh garment industry
Source: BGMEA (2020).

Bangladesh RMG is that there is no concrete evidence of the total number of garment workers. Without any research, the BGMEA shows on its website that the size of workers is 4 million. There was no change of the number of workers for several years which indicates that the size of workers was based on assumption or old data. However, the Government's labour force survey finds 3.3 million workers in the RMG industry. After the Rana Plaza, it is also a major concern to produce a database of workers and the BGMEA has started a project on a biometric database of workers but it has not completed yet although started five years ago.[5]

Although the contribution of woven ($1,240.48 million) was much higher than knit ($204.54 million) in 1992–1993, the gap has narrowed a lot in 2019–2020; woven accounts for $14,041.19 million, and knit accounts for $13,908 million (BGMEA, 2020). The major exporting garments are shirts, trousers, jackets, t-shirts, and sweaters. Among them, the largest share of export earning comes from trousers and t-shirts: $6,389.38 million and $6,292.25 million, respectively (BGMEA, 2020). The EU and the U.S. are the two traditional and dominant markets of the Bangladesh RMG's export. In 2019, 61.75% of Bangladesh RMG's total exports reached the EU countries, and 18.20% reached the U.S., 3.37% reached Canada, and 16.68% reached the non-traditional countries (BGMEA, 2020). The top importers in the EU are France, Italy, Germany, the U.K., and Spain. Data on the direction of exports indicates a gradual shift from the traditional market (8.7% growth) to non-traditional markets (11% growth). Of the major non-traditional destinations, exports to Australia, Japan, and India posted notable growth recently.

Policies also play a significant role in the successful number of exports throughout the global space. To illustrate this, we can take the example of policies regarding quotas and trade access. As Bangladesh is labelled as an LDC, it enjoys more benefits under the EU's Generalized Scheme of

Table 2.1 Growth of garments industry and employment

Indicators	*No. of garment factories*	*Factory growth rate %*	*Workers (in mil)*	*Workers growth rate %*
1984–1985	384	–	0.12	–
1985–1986	594	54.69	0.2	66.67
1986–1987	629	5.89	0.28	40
1987–1988	685	8.9	0.31	10.71
1988–1989	725	5.84	0.32	3.23
1989–1990	759	4.69	0.34	6.25
1990–1991	834	9.88	0.4	17.65
1991–1992	1,163	39.45	0.58	45
1992–1993	1,537	32.16	0.8	37.93
1993–1994	1,839	19.65	0.83	3.75
1994–1995	2,182	18.65	1.2	44.58
1995–1996	2,353	7.84	1.29	7.5
1996–1997	2,503	6.37	1.3	0.78
1997–1998	2,726	8.91	1.5	15.38
1998–1999	2,963	8.69	1.5	0.0
1999–2000	3,200	8.o	1.6	6.67
2000–2001	3,480	8.75	1.8	12.5
2001–2002	3,618	3.97	1.8	0.0
2002–2003	3,760	3.92	2.0	11.11
2003–2004	3,957	5.24	2.0	0.0
2004–2005	4,107	3.79	2.0	0.0
2005–2006	4,220	2.75	2.2	10
2006–2007	4,490	6.4	2.4	9.09
2007–2008	4,743	5.63	2.8	16.67
2008–2009	4,825	1.73	3.1	10.71
2010–2011	5,150	–	3.6	–
2012–2013	5,876	–	4.0	–
2013–2014	4,222	–	4.0	–
2016–2017	4,482	–	–	–
2018–2019	4,621	–	–	–

Source: BGMEA (2020).

Table 2.2 Distribution of major clients based on factory size

Major clients	*Factory size*	
	Large	*Medium*
Brand	14 (53.85)	51 (60)
Brand + retailer	11 (42.31)	29 (34.12)
Retailer	0 (0)	2 (2.35)
Buying house	0 (0)	1 (1.18)
Brand + buying house	0 (0)	2 (2.35)
Retailer + buying house	0 (0)	0 (0)
Brand + retailer + buying house	1 (3.85)	0 (0)
Total	26 (100)	85 (100)

Source: CPD (2018).
Note: Figures in parenthesis indicate column percentage.

Preferences (GSP) trade system and the Everything But Arms (EBA) arrangement. This arrangement provides a duty-free quota and free access to the EU for exports for all products except arms and ammunition (European Commission, 2015). This has had a significant impact on earnings through export, especially during the policy's consolidation between 2010 and 2011.

The buying and selling are maintained either directly from buyers or indirectly through buying houses, which produce for the local market as well as act as intermediaries for large to medium international retailers such as Walmart, H&M, and JCPenney. Below is a list of top retailers and fashion brands that currently import from Bangladesh, according to BKMEA/BGMEA – Some of these retailers directly source from Bangladesh, and have local offices. The presence of international networks via offices allows for direct control of capacity and supply chain management. According to CPD (2018) about 61% of the factories do business with a brand, and 30% do so with brand and retailer (Table 2.2).

Table 2.3 RMG exports of Bangladesh

Year	*RMG export (mil $)*	*Total export (mil $)*	*RMG export as % of total export*
1983–1984	31.57	811	3.89
1988–1989	471.09	1,291.56	36.47
1994–1995	2,228.35	3,472.56	64.17
2000–2001	4,859.83	6,467.3	75.14
2006–2007	9,211.23	12,177.86	75.64
2007–2008	10,699.8	14,110.8	75.83
2008–2009	12,347.77	15,565.19	79.33
2012–2013	21,515.73	27,027.36	79.61
2013–2014	24,491.88	30,186.62	81.13
2016–2017	28,149.84	34,655.90	81.23
2018–2019	34,133.27	40,535.04	84.21
2019–2020	27,949.19	33,674.09	83.00

Source: BGMEA (2020).

Box 2.2 Leading buyers of Bangladesh RMG

GAP (U.S.) K-mart (U.S.) M&S (U.K.) Li & Fung (Hong Kong)
H&M (Sweden) Wal-Mart (U.S.) PVH (U.S.) Adidas (Germany)
Levi's (U.S.) VF Asia (U.S.) Nike (U.S.) Puma (Germany)
Tesco (U.K.) C&A (Germany) Target (U.S.) ASDA (U.K.)
Next (U.K.) Zara (Spain) Old Navy (U.S.) S. Oliver (Germany)

Source: Author prepared from different websites.

2.3 Economic and social impact

One way to evaluate the economic impact of the garment industry is to compare the export share of garments to other export items. The main export items of Bangladesh are garments, jute and jute goods, tea, leather, frozen food, and ceramic tableware. Among these, garments are the key export sector; the share of garments in total exports was only 0.42% in 1980, while the rest of the products contributed more than 99% of total exports (EPB, 2006). Within ten years, garments became the principal export sector of the country with an export share of 42.8% in 1990. The contribution of garments in exports has been increasing since the emergence of this industry while the export share of other products has been declining. The combined share of products excepting garments declined from 99.58% in 1980 to 26.5% in 2003. In contrast, the share of garments to total exports increased from almost nothing in 1980 to 79% by the end of 2009.

A direct impact of the garment industry on Bangladesh's economy is to be seen in the contribution of garment exports to Bangladesh's Gross Domestic Product (GDP). In their study, Islam and Quddus (1996) found that the contribution of total exports to GDP was 5.8% 1976–1977 and increased to 7.6% in 1990–1991. The RMG's contribution to GDP has increased from almost nothing in 1976–1977 to about 3.5% in 1990–1991 and 11.17% in 2017–2018. Export earnings were less than 1 million in the 1970s but rose to U.S.$2,228.35 million in 1994–1995, and by the end of 2018–2019, export earnings were U.S.$34,133.27 million (Table 2.3).

The garment sector absorbed nearly one-fifth of the women employed in the manufacturing sector (Zohir and Paul-Majumder, 1996). The involvement of these garment workers in the paid labour market has had an impact on poverty. Kabeer and Mahmud (2004) established a relationship between women's employment in the garment industry and levels of household poverty. The first aspect of this relationship is that the emergence of the garment industry has generated paid job opportunities for women who had not participated in the paid labour market for a long time. These are the women workers who entered the paid labour market for the first time. After surveying 1,322 women workers and their households, Kabeer and Mahmud (2004) concluded that their average monthly income was almost double the monthly per capita "poverty line" income. This indicates that their monthly income could support at least one other adult or two children and their earnings never fell below the poverty line income. The second aspect of the relationship between women's employment and poverty, as outlined by the authors, is that these women garment workers earned sufficient money to meet their basic needs and to support other family members in the form of sending remittance to relatives living in villages.

Perhaps most importantly, the development of the garment industry has triggered a social change in Bangladesh by generating considerable female employment outside the family unit. This has made women not only visible in the labour market but also empowered in society. Ever since the emergence of the garment industry as the major employer of the female labour force, women have challenged social restrictions in society. Nowadays, a common scene in the early morning for the two major cities of Bangladesh – Dhaka, and Chittagong – is of thousands of women going to the garment factories. This is a scene that could not be imagined two decades ago. The advent of the garment industry has therefore caused a noticeable social change in the life of women in Bangladesh, and therefore of the society as a whole.

A nation's development may be difficult to achieve without the opportunity for the full participation of women in the labour market. It is particularly true where manpower is one of the resources of a densely populated country. For instance, the population is increasing at an alarming rate in Bangladesh and women comprise almost half of its population. But the participation of women in the paid labour market has been negligible. Women's share of total paid employment was only 5% in 1967 (World Bank, 1990). Failure to integrate women into the industries and programmes associated with economic development has been a crucial problem since Bangladeshi independence. The situation for women was worse before the 1980s. To understand the reasons for this exclusion, we need to study Bangladeshi culture and society. The lives of Bangladeshi women have been dominated by a patriarchal, patrilineal, and patrilocal social system (ADB, 2001). The general attitude of society is that men do all the productive work and women are entirely dependent on them (Khan, 1988). The prescribed woman's role includes maintenance of the family, childrearing, and other domestic activities. Besides these functions, in rural Bangladesh, women also help their families in processing crops after cultivation. Until the recent past, women were physically confined to their homes and excluded from the public sphere of fields, markets, roads, and towns (Chen, 1995). A sharp sexual division of labour is established through socio-economic inequality and this inequality permeates every aspect of women's lives.

Although Chen argues that NGOs' activities have promoted women's participation in the labour market significantly, Kabeer (2000) believes that despite the expansion of NGO efforts, the direct impact of NGOs on women's labour force participation remained marginal. Kabeer also suggests that the advent of the garment manufacturing industry has taken women to the labour market on a large scale with sufficient visibility after a decade of government and non-government efforts had failed. It has helped to create a new industrial working class in the country. The garment sector mushroomed in the cities and is a major factor behind the changing pattern of female labour force participation. We turn now to exploring the reasons for this phenomenon.

As noted above, women now constitute the major workforce in Bangladesh's export-oriented garment industry. Some gender-related factors are influential in encouraging garment employers to employ more women than men (Paul-Majumder and Begum, 2000). According to Paul-Majumder and Begum, employers see women as more controllable, less mobile, and less likely to join a trade union than men, and believe women can do better in sewing because this coincides with their traditional jobs. In a study where she explored the reasons for employers' preference for female labour, Kabeer (2000) interviewed some garment employers:

> Men in groups will immediately start agitating for more pay. Women go straight home after work because of domestic responsibilities or because it gets dark. Women listen better and they don't talk back. Men won't take instructions or accept authority easily. And women are cheaper because they have fewer choices – in terms of the physical location of work and in terms of their physical ability to do different kinds of work.
>
> (Kabeer, 2000: 71–72)

Kabeer (2000) has identified four groups of women who have entered the garment industry. One group of women came from poor households, working in domestic service or small workshops or factory units before joining the garment industry. The second group chose garment jobs in response to some specific adversity such as the death of their husband or father, divorce, or collapse of the family business. The third group of women entered this job as a way of improving their living standards or for their children's prospects. The fourth group of women explained their entry in terms of earning for their own needs such as saving money for their dowry. It is true for all four groups that garment employment was preferable to other forms of employment available to women of their class and has had an impact on changing their societal status (Kabeer, 2000).

The impact of female involvement in the garment industry has been momentous. Jobs at garment factories have not only given workers present financial security but also a sense of security for the future (Paul-Majumder and Zohir, 1994). Paul-Majumder and Zohir further state that wage employment in the garment industry has influenced culturally-bound women to live away from families and enabled married workers to share domestic chores with their husbands. Employment empowers women in terms of making decisions such as choosing a marriage partner. The decision to enter the industry has provided an opportunity to take care of oneself financially and build one's future which has reduced the burden and responsibility of the family for one's well-being (Kibria, 2002). And so, the traditional role of women bearing children and maintaining household affairs has changed remarkably. Women are working hard not only for their satisfaction but also for a better future for their children. The standard and diversity of household diets have improved. The traditional, dominating role of family and society towards women has changed and women have achieved a more autonomous societal status. Paul-Majumder and Zohir (1994) have found that paid employment has a very favourable impact on women's social prestige in society, conjugal life, matrimonial relationship, fertility and age at marriage, decision-making, and other aspects of life. The nature and social image of garment work tend to hold some attractions over traditional earnings activities in villages such as threshing rice, weaving baskets, raising livestock, and growing vegetables (Kibria, 2002). In general, garment work is seen as modern which carries social prestige for the workers. The expansion of the manufacturing sector and especially the garment industry is one of the key elements in Bangladesh's urbanization and migration processes (Afsar, 2002). This industry has generated significant employment in the urban sector. As noted above, the majority of the companies exporting garments are located in two cities – Dhaka and Chittagong. Before the emergence of the garment industry, these two cities were occupied by important government and private offices as well as residences from different classes of families. The garment factories appeared – without any concrete plan – in the centre of these cities and even in residential areas. There is little hard data on the impact of the addition of more than a million workers to both cities (Harris, 1999). Harris (1999) also found that the proportion of migrant workers increased from 31% in 1981–1990 to 60% in 1991–1996 for males, and from 28% in 1981–1990 to 64% in 1991–1996 for females. Due to the migration of garment workers, the urban population has increased, slums have spread, urban utilities and services have been placed under pressure and the cities have become congested. One of the effects of migration on women is that the living standards of women garment workers have been improved since their involvement in the garment industry, as is evidenced by a study conducted by Hewett and Amin (2000). Their research demonstrates that women garment workers have maintained higher living conditions than women living traditional lifestyles. The study's indicators of living standards include the quality of housing, the existence of piped water in the household, the availability of sanitary latrines, and the density of living arrangements. The authors found that garment workers have higher-quality housing conditions and access to modern infrastructures, such as electricity, clean drinking water, and sanitation services, than women in rural areas. The researchers also conclude that whereas almost no women in villages have access to piped water, and one in ten has access to hygienic toilets, these services are available to more than four-fifths of garment workers. At the same time, one adverse effect of migration is that garment workers are likely to reside in more crowded housing situations – sometimes more than five people in a room. Sometimes women garment workers live with their relatives or family members, which ensures their protection. Family-based living arrangements not only protect them but also provide necessary services such as child care (Afsar, 2002).

In a male-dominated society like Bangladesh, the decision to choose a partner is centred on the opinions of male family members. In some cases, all family members sit together and decide on choosing a marriage partner for any member of the family. There is no space for personal decision in this regard and it is more acute for a female who has limited power to choose her own partner. This form of social control has changed for garment workers – though not significantly. However, what is significant is that entry into garment work gives women the opportunity of delaying marriage and child-bearing. Nowadays, female workers feel freer to discuss sexual problems with their doctors. Hewett and Amin (2000) found that more than a quarter of all garment workers remain unmarried by age 24, whereas marriage is universal in villages by this age.

Another social impact of the growth of employment in the garment industry is that due to their emerging autonomy married garment workers are controlling their fertility more effectively than Bangladeshi women in general (Afsar, 2002). By comparing different studies conducted for examining reproductive behaviour, it is evident that, according to the Bangladesh Demographic and Health Survey data, married women of reproductive age have on average 2.4 children. This figure, as the author argues, for garment workers (based on a sample survey of garment factory workers) is lower – between 1.2 and 0.8 since awareness of using contraception is widespread among garment workers. Delayed marriage and effective control of fertility by garment workers have played a major role in decreasing the country's population growth.

From this discussion, we can conclude that women workers have become empowered after joining the garment factories. The number of women employees has increased; their lives are better than others working in other industries; society has embraced them with respect and dignity; and, above all, they are more conscious of their rights. However, one area of empowerment is still missing and it is upward social mobility. The overwhelming majority of female workers are employed in the lower grade of their jobs, and very few are working in the upper levels or decision-making positions, such as supervisor or manager. They still need to work a lot in taking the leadership role as is explained by a union leader below.

Box 2.3 A female union leader's views on female leadership role

Still, now the active participation of women in workers union is very low. It is hard to calculate the percentage. What we are thinking is that it is true that we didn't put much importance on the issue before Rana Plaza. But now we are thinking about this as there are 80% of female workers. If we fail to organize these women, leadership will not develop. From our organization, we especially emphasize women's participation. We provide all the facilities that women need to come to the organization. However, still, now, women's participation is much less, everywhere in society.

In the movement among the workers in 2017 and before that in 2014 and 2010 there was women participation. When wages increased in 2010, women came forward. This was not the case in 2006, maybe they would be at the front for two days, but later they would go home. Women were used as a decorative part of the protest. It was also a common conception that no one will hit women, so they were put in front. Now, considering the wage and everything, it is difficult for garment workers to survive. As life becomes tough, men and women have to come to the factory and in the movement, still, very few women are coming in a leadership role. When the wage increased in 2013 and 2014, overall workers were afraid. Now, that fear is much less, compared to previous times. In 2017, when we organized the movement, the number of workers that attended was surprising for us. This is a good sign. This depends on the organizers.

In our country, everywhere one sees, from politics to economics to policymaking, women's participation is less. To improve this condition, women and worker protests need to be strong. When women will understand their position, when they will realize their self-respect, women on their own will come to the movement. Different situations will bring them forward. The garment is not different from others, but as women are more in number in garment sectors, it would have been natural if more women came forward. Women who work in factories are much overloaded compared to their men counterparts. Women workers are getting home around 8, 10, or 11 at night. After getting home, they have to cook for their family. In many places gas supply is absent, so women who have to cook have to wake up at dawn. The women workers get less sleep than male workers.

As now women are earning, their importance has increased a little inside the family. But still, now, they are unable to play the decision-making role in the family. In a family, maybe the husband and wife both are working in the garments factory. The wife would have to take care of the child and do all other household work due to her being a woman. Women have to take the extra burden for their being women.

Male might not want women to come into leadership, but nothing depends on the male's desire. If I want to be a leader or not, no male will decide but in our society, women have to face many obstacles. Whoever's husband is in the organization, maybe the wife can't take part in the organization. A single woman can be more involved in the organization. Many factors work behind this. Thus, the number of women in organizations is very few. Factory owners assume that women will talk less and will not protest. Any problem is created by the male. Women do not understand math, will shut up if abused. The situation is changing now. The change is not that big, but women are coming to the organization.

Even in 2010, when I was not working about workers protest, at that time, if there is any protest or event, women would leave the place slowly. Or women are leaving when it comes to coming in contact with the police. Women in garments practice veil so that people respect their profession since there was a negative assumption about women garment workers in people's perception. In 2010–2011 I observed that there are few changes. Women are coming forward. When police are trying to make the workers scattered, maybe many men have fled from the place, but a woman is crashing with the police. I still remember a girl name Rahela, whose picture appeared in newspapers. Police were throwing tear gas, and everybody was fleeing, but two girls were still there, arguing with the police. Then the police hit one of them on the head. I wrote a piece on this entitled "*Lakho Rahelar opekkhay* Bangladesh."

Vulnerable people might be silent at first, but gradually they come out of their silence. The Labour minister says that they want a women's union, and if there is one the organization will sanction the union immediately, but women are not coming forward. We had a meeting in Ashuliya last week. We are feeling good that in our 21 member committee, we have 5/6 women members. The women members couldn't talk previously, but now they are coming out as leaders. This was not possible seven years back. Finding a woman leader was much more difficult. The reason for them coming out as protestors or leaders is their vulnerable position. They do not have the option of being shy. They have to come to the movement. One can see a female head in many organizations, but not in mid-level management. Let's take our organization. We have 23 members on our central committee. Among them four are women. Even the woman coming from the middle class is also less in our organization. They are also fewer in numbers in politics. As women are the most deprived, they have to face sexual harassment in the factory, they get paid less. So women will remain silent for a time being, but not for a long time Suppose at home, you are beating your wife. She will remain silent for a few days maybe. If she has minimum self-respect then she will protest.

Various NGOs and organizations are working on these issues. Importance was given to three things – wage, safety, and trade union. New issues include questions about why there are fewer women members, or why they are unable to come to the leadership. A workshop will be held on the relations between men and women. The workshop covers the issues that women are not coming into organizations or talking about sexual harassment, which is part of the fourth priority or interest in the workshop. When Tazrin happened, people didn't talk about wages but about safety. Safety then became the number one priority.

Women need to be given a certain space so that they can hone their skills before they can begin working, as it is seen that they do not have the qualifications to make it as an organizer or committee member. Thus they need to be inspired and this is one of the tasks that members of the worker organizations need to undertake especially since the female participation level is quite low and they avoid joining on their own for various reasons.

Source: Interview taken by the author on the 14th of February 2018.

2.4 Hidden cost of RMG's development

The RMG industry in Bangladesh is well known for its failure to ensure the safety of workers at workplaces. Incidents of factory fires at Saraka Garments in 1990; Florence Fabric, Nouvelle and Modern Garments in 1997; Chowdhury Knitwear in 2000; and Tazreen Garments in 2012 killed more than 201 workers, most of whom were young women (Rahman and Rahman, 2020). And finally, on 24th of April 2013, Rana Plaza, an eight-storey building housing five garment factories, collapsed, causing more than 1,100 workers to lose their lives and nearly 2,600 to be injured. After noticing a crack, the workers initially refused to enter the building, but they were threatened with dismissal and forced back inside. The sufferings can be summarized in the reporting of Al Jazeera (2014). Laboni, a female worker in a garment factory of Rana Plaza, was buried under a pile of rubble and the rescuers had to cut off her left arm to save her life. The traumatized Laboni does not work anymore and went back to her village for good relying on a mechanical prosthetic limb. This worst industrial disaster of the world devastated the lives of thousands of workers and their families.

Another social cost of the success stories of the Bangladesh RMG is the constant deterioration of the workers' health as Neve and Prentise (2017: 3) argued, "But far more pervasive – and invisible – is the violation of workers' health on a day-to-day basis." Paul-Majumder's (2001) study discloses that 90% of garment workers have experienced illness or disease during the month before the researcher's interviews with them. The more common diseases were headache, anaemia, fever, chest, stomach, eye and ear pain, cough and cold, diarrhoea, dysentery, urinary tract infection, and reproductive health problems. Employees suffered from different kinds of diseases after working in garment factories. To establish a relationship between these diseases and occupational hazards, Paul-Majumder analyzed the health status of employees before and after entering the garment workforce. After the analysis, the author found that approximately 75% of the workers were in good health before they joined the garment factory. The causes of health deterioration were occupational hazards, adverse working conditions, absence of staff amenities, stringent terms and conditions of garment employment, workplace stress, and poor wages.

From the above discussion of the garment industry's general working conditions, we can determine that the working conditions of most Third World countries, like Bangladesh, resemble the earlier development of garment production in First World countries, where garment workers were vulnerable. Robert (1983: 31) suggests: "the conditions of employment in many (not necessarily) textiles and clothing factories in the developing countries hark back to those found in the nineteenth-century in Europe and North America." In developing countries, the textile and clothing industry employs predominantly young female workers in conditions that recall those of the sweatshops and mills of nineteenth-century Europe and North America (Dicken, 1998). Bair, Anner and Blasi (2017) also agree with Robert finding a similar structure of the organization of production between New York's early-twentieth-century garment industry and today's global production network.

However, a recent survey of 1,500 workers by Kabeer et al. (2020) finds better working conditions in the industry compared to the past (see Box 2.4). The findings summary of this study is as follows. Average basic salaries were higher than the prevailing minimum wage, over 90% of workers reported that they had permanent status, ID cards, paid leave, maternity leave. According to the survey, 95% of workers felt safe working in their present factory since the formation of the Health and Safety committee in their factories and receiving training on health and safety. Compared to the 1980s, far better-working conditions exist now in most of the workplaces, particularly in medium and large factories. It has been possible because of the pressure from the global union to abolish child labour, the ILO's monitoring to maintain core labour standards, the compliance conditionality of development partners, the awareness campaigns of local unions and NGOs,

Box 2.4 Workers' outcome standards

- Workers reported an average basic salary of 7,200 takas per month
- Workers reported an average working day of 8 hours
- Workers reported busy period overtime levels involving over 3.3 hours per day
- 62% of workers have written contracts
- 97% of workers have permanent status
- 91% of workers reported entitlement to paid leave
- 90% of workers reported entitlement to maternity leave
- 90% of workers reported that their factories had Health and Safety Committees
- 95% of workers believed their factories to be safe
- 90% of workers asserted that they would not enter a factory building if they believed it to be unsafe
- Workers report average job tenure of 3.6 years
- >73% of workers from Accord-Alliance affiliated factories and 80% of workers from unaffiliated factories reported experiencing abuse and mistreatment at their current factory
- >57% of workers reported improvements in supervisor behaviour since Rana Plaza

Source: Schüßler et al. (2019).

the buyers' code of conduct, and the third-party audit system (Rahman and Rahman, 2020).

Despite these achievements mainly due to the initiatives are taken after the Rana Plaza disaster, the availability of the cheapest labour in the world is the selling point of the industry (Table 2.4). For more than two decades, the minimum wage of workers was less than 1,000 taka (about $12) per month. After labour unrest, the government increased the minimum wage in 2010 to Tk. 3,000 ($43). Thousands of workers took to the streets in July 2010, burning cars and blocking traffic to protest against this decision, which fell far short of their demands. Whereas the increase in the minimum wage was supposed to please garment workers, the increased wage still did not meet their daily consumption needs in the city. After momentous pressure from trade unions, the garment factory owners accepted a new minimum wage proposed by the government: Tk. 5,300 ($68) after the Rana Plaza. In its response to the demands for an increase in the minimum wage, the Bangladeshi government considered the contributions of the workers as well as the dependency of the country on this industry. In response to continuous labour unrest, the government finally declared a new pay structure in 2018,

Table 2.4 Changing wage structure: 2006–2018

Grade	*2006 (Tk)*	*2010 (Tk)*	*Increase over 2006 (%)*	*2013 (Tk)*	*Increase over 2010 (%)*	*2018 (Tk)*	*Increase over 2013 (%)*
Grade 1	5,140	9,300	80.93	13,000	39.87	18,257	40.44
Grade 2	3,840	7,200	87.50	10,900	51.38	15,416	41.43
Grade 3	2,449	4,120	68.23	6,805	65.16	9,875	44.67
Grade 4	2,250	3,763	67.24	6,420	70.60	9,347	45.59
Grade 5	2,046	3,455	68.87	6,042	74.87	8,875	46.89
Grade 6	1,851	3,210	73.42	5,678	76.88	8,420	48.29
Grade 7	1,662	3,000	80.45	5,300	76.66	8,000	50.49

Source: Rahman (2019).

and the minimum wage was set at Tk. 8,000 ($100). The increase is perhaps best attributed to international pressure and the efforts of the labour wing. Bangladesh still offers the lowest minimum wage in the world. In recent days, the concern is not the minimum wage but the living wage. The living wage of workers in Dhaka satellite town should be Tk. 13,630 and in Dhaka city Tk. 16,460 (Living Wage Benchmark Report, 2016). At least from this report's calculation, the current minimum wage is 43 to 51% of the living wage. There has been a widening gap between employees' minimum wage and the rising price of essential commodities. This makes it quite impossible for workers to meet their daily needs. The Bangladeshi government has not been able to offer a liveable standard minimum wage and control commodity prices. The minimum wage needs to be framed in the light of present daily expenditure costs.

To sum up, the garment workers migrated to cities to work in factories. The initial stage of their migration was usually not as pleasant as they struggled to cope with the urban environment. They were apprehensive about interacting with people, understanding the responsibility of their jobs, running the sewing machines, and, above all, feeling free to work in an environment that was entirely different from village life. But their determination to become empowered and be respected in society allowed them to gradually overcome these challenges. The jobs in the garment industry have become a source of subsistence and inspiration. Their involvement in the industry has become so precious for these women that they are ready to sacrifice just about anything in their lives to protect their jobs because they know that no other employment is available for them and that this kind of occupation is the one that is most suitable for them. Garment employers are also acquainted with the belief that these workers are vulnerable and protect their jobs at any cost even if they face adverse working conditions. Their vulnerability is experienced in two ways. First, garment workers are vulnerable to the adverse working conditions in the garment factories. They are prepared to work in poor conditions because they need their jobs. If they quit their jobs in the garment sector, it is very difficult to secure other employment as the job market for women is very limited. The only "solution" is for these employees to continue with their jobs whatever the existing working conditions may be, and these workers are vulnerable in this sense. Second, worker vulnerability is not only limited to working conditions but also to the threat of losing their jobs at any time. The future of these garment workers is under threat as the garment factories are struggling to survive due to the adverse effects of globalization. There are no alternative employment options for workers who have lost their jobs. The workers who are still employed in garment factories are scared of losing their jobs at any time. Although these garment employees work very hard, their fate is not in their own hands but in the hands of the key actors in the global market.

Notes

1 In 1796, 65 tons of jute fibre was exported to England, 40 tons to Germany and 6 tons to the U.S. During this period, hand-woven jute goods were finding export markets in Britain, Germany, France, North and South America, Burma, Java, China, Australia, and Africa. Exports of these handloom fabrics amounted to 9,035,713 pieces in 1850. (Ahmad, 1976)

2 Choi, Chung and Marian (1985) conclude that the terms and conditions of the MFA deviated from the GATT in two fundamental ways: first, the provisions of GATT prohibited the use of quantitative restrictions on imports or exports; second, the MFA allowed for discriminatory treatment, which was the most serious convention of GATT's Most Favoured Nation (MFN) principle: MFN means treating one's trading partners equally on the principle of non-discrimination; under GATT, if a country allows foreign competition in a sector, equal opportunities in that sector should be given to service providers from all other GATT members.

3 These are used in international and domestic trade. The parties to a BB/LC are: the buyer and their bank, the seller/manufacturer and their bank, and the manufacturer's supplier and their bank. This type of documentary credit transaction is used when a seller/manufacturer has to purchase a component but may not have the cash flow to do so. For instance, the owner of a garment company in Bangladesh gets an order from a buyer and needs to import materials that are not available in the local market. In this situation, the buyer opens a LC in a local bank that guarantees the payment of the export and the bank informs the exporter about the LC. The Bangladeshi entrepreneur then opens another LC with a local bank to import the materials and does not need to spend money. The buyer or any other supplier sends the shipment of these materials to the Bangladeshi garment owner. After receiving the imported materials, the entrepreneur produces the garments and sends them to the buyer. The owner of the garment company receives the amount of the export minus the cost of the import and the bank's commission. The bank also supplies the cost of imports to the buyer or supplier.

4 The Centre for Entrepreneurship and Development (CED) of BRAC University has started a project recently to explore the number of export oriented garment factories in Bangladesh. The project is known as MiB, funded by Laudes Foundation and the object ive is digital mapping of factories i.e. digitally can locate the factory and some basic information of that factory. The project details can be found at https://mappedinbangladesh.org/

5 The reasons of slow progress of this project is available at https://www.thedailystar.net/business/rmg-workers-database-not-ready-even-after-5yrs-1567972.

3 From first-generation to second-generation entrepreneurs

3.1 First-generation entrepreneurs

When the garment industry started its journey in 1978, conditions were not favourable for manufacturers except for the quota system. The entrepreneurs encountered a government policy that discouraged exports, high prices for importing raw materials, uncountable bureaucratic problems, unavailability of modern technology, and most importantly, lack of experience in the garment industry. This was a challenging task for early manufacturers who took the risk and invested in the export business. Under these conditions, a small group of businesspeople who had a close connection with the government and also had a healthy amount of capital started exporting garment products in the late 1970s. There is no doubt that this group of manufacturers was taking risks in spite of having no experience in the garment industry. However, they were influential in changing governmental policy. When these manufacturers endured the challenges and were able to make profits, the second group of garment manufacturers appeared in the 1980s who were employees in the garment factories of the earlier group of entrepreneurs. Having gained experience in the garment business, these employees left their jobs and established their own garment companies. They were young, hardworking, had a small amount of capital, and upheld the dynamic spirit for making profits by utilizing their experience. The third group of garment manufacturers came on the scene in the 1990s when the industry became stable and was already in good shape. At that time, the prevailing thought was that the garment industry was a way of making huge profits within a short period. At this stage, people from different backgrounds became involved in this business. In this book, these three groups together are considered as "first-generation entrepreneurs."

In their survey, Quddus and Rashid (2000) found that most of the garment manufacturers in Bangladesh are young, educated, and have come from diverse backgrounds – the bureaucracy, the army, trading, export, and the manufacturing business. According to Quddus and Rashid (2000: 91):

> In Bangladesh, a major change has occurred in the industrial scene in the nature and quality of entrepreneurial talent due to the booming

> apparel industry. Members of the elite middle class, individuals from various 'respected' professions – university professors, army generals, ex-secretaries and ministers – all are represented in this industry.

A statement from Amin, the General Secretary of National Garment Workers Federation characterizes the nature of garment manufacturers in Bangladesh:

> A good portion of the employers lacks consciousness. What class do they belong to? Are they from the upper class or the old generation or the new generation? Some of the employers are now parliament members. Some of them are ex-minister, army officials, and civil servants. You can find some are in this business in the flow of generation. Their earlier generation was in industry-related occupation. But the number is few. At present most of the employers are new in this industry who has limited knowledge or experience about industrialization, labor handling and the production market. For garment, you don't need a healthy amount of investment. Generally, the employers run this business by taking a loan from a bank. You can't get the exact nature of industrialization here.[1]

The above-mentioned characteristics of the first-generation owners are reflected in the starting journey of four garment entrepreneurs presented below.[2]

When Muhammad Saidur Rahman founded his export-oriented garment company "Bantai Industries Private Limited" in 1990, in many ways, he was typical of the new garment entrepreneurs who started up companies during the previous decade of industrial expansion: he had no prior experience in the industry. Instead, Rahman possessed over two decades of experience working for relief and development agencies in Bangladesh, including the Red Cross and Oxfam, before moving into the garment business. He started his life as a teacher and, after Bangladesh's independence, began working for the Red Cross in 1972. He remained with the Red Cross for nine years, becoming Oxfam's Country Director during his subsequent 11-year stint with that NGO. After the completion of his Oxfam position, Rahman set up a business that allowed him to pursue a two-pronged goal, combining business and social engagement. It was a joint-venture company with a foreign partner. As the Taiwanese partner was responsible for marketing, Rahman oversaw the production side. He held a 51% share while 49% was held by the Taiwanese partner. Rahman had convinced his Taiwanese partner to accept the social programmes he wanted to introduce into the factory. He was motivated to do something for the poor which was something he had been doing all his life. Besides prospering, the goal of the founder was to empower the employees by offering good workplace practices and other incentives. Rahman outlined the goals of the company as follows:

> Any effort that will empower the workers is best practice. Welfare is the vehicle; it's not the aim to me. Other factories may have medical or day-care; they think it's their aim. But my objective is empowerment through all these programmes. Other factories' aim is service delivery. But it has no achievement in the long run. Suppose you provide air condition in the factory, but when they return home husband[s] torture their wives. So what is the benefit of it? I want to make a workforce who can face exploitative force in society.[3]

While Rahman's NGO experiences drove him to empower vulnerable people through a garment factory with a foreign partner, another entrepreneur, Shaon Das started his company "Texphin Garments" with local partners. Besides graduation from a prestigious institution, the Institute of Business Administration of Dhaka University, he elicits the traits of a passionate and driven entrepreneur, with creative skills obtained from observation and experience. In his final year at Dhaka University, Das and his friend Rafiqul were appointed by a senior of his university to oversee the production of two companies in 1993. The main problem of these companies was very low production. Since the companies belonged to the first generation of garments factories, the owners and employees had very little idea about how to run the factory efficiently and thus propel them towards a successful establishment in the global network. At this time, Das and his friend went to the factory and observed the production line in between classes, and they were committed to the task. Before this project, they had to extensively study the garment factories and management styles as this knowledge was far from available in the 1980s. Eventually, after three to four days of observation, the two friends came up with a way to arrange the production lines. There were eight lines with about 22 people in each. They requested that one of the lines be organized the way they thought would be more efficient, and the managers granted them to do so. At the end of the week, it turned out that the single line they had rearranged had increased the production by at least 5% and so all the lines were rearranged as per their model. They then visited the factories and updated the inventory management style and the record-keeping, and all these eventually resulted in avoiding the rampant theft of company property that had been occurring until then. For their work they received Tk. 30,000 since the manager had been so impressed with the output. The success of this endeavour motivated Das and his friend to start a consultancy service for the garment industry.

However, the absence of consulting culture for factory management in the country in the 1980s pushed Das to a banking career at Sonali Bank with a salary of Tk. 11,000 per month. He was in charge of providing credit to a potential business project by overseeing the fact that the businesses would buy appropriate machinery and other resources required to set up a factory. Das was authorized to sanction up to Tk. 25 lacs which is equivalent to today's

Tk. 300 crores. Eventually, though, he had left the job because he didn't get his desired position in the bank.

Since Das knew about setting up a factory he continued to provide consultancy service informally. He helped out Saha in starting up the first polythene bag factory in Bangladesh, which had faced a lot of obstacles just because no one understood the utility of the bags. Saha was so grateful to Das that he wanted to do something for Das. It was then that Saha came up with the plan to start an export-oriented garment company with Das. They set up a factory in Kamalapur with an investment of Tk. 3 lacs and the first subcontract order was 10,000 pieces.

Whereas Das started his career as a banker and a casual consultant and later founded a garment company with a local partner, the journey of another garment owner, Nuru Alam was a different story. From the very beginning, Alam was a businessman based in Chattogram. His first business was a tyre tube, on which he partnered with three of his friends who returned from Germany. At that time Alam was the president of the tyre tube business association. But Alam's partners did not like the business and all of them shifted to Dhaka to grab an opportunity. A sick garment factory was about to be sold by a local Bank for about Tk. one crore because its owner, who was a minister, could not run it. Alam and his friends discussed the matter seriously and bought this factory from the bank and started the business as a subcontract factory. Alam had four partners, and initially, they invested around Tk. 10 lac per partner. Though the business started in 1995, Nuru Alam came to Dhaka to settle for the business in 1998. Initially, Alam started with a little project but gradually his business started to rise from a subcontractor to direct supplier to buyer. Within 18 months they paid their debts to the Bank. After the dept was cleared, the Bank encouraged Alam to expand his business. He took the advice and expanded his business to include more units, lines, and workers. But Alam and the business got a shock when his friend and the MD of the company died in 2007. Another friend and business partner became sick. Before the demise of a partner and illness of another partner, Alam bought a huge area of about 40 *bigha* and 40,000 square feet in Mirzapur. Still, there was an immense opportunity to expand more since the volume of the order was continuously growing up. It was required to increase the factory buildings and dyeing capacity. To increase the overall capacity of the company, Alam partnered with a large company. The merging was a great decision because the per line production capacity was increased from 10 tonnes to 35 tonnes, factory area from 40 to 150 bigha, size 40,000 to 500,000 square feet, 1 to 8 buildings, business value from 200 to 1,000 crore. In the beginning, the size of the workforce was 500. Now, it has increased to 10,000. Alam started the company with a capacity of 50,000 pieces of garments per month and now his capacity is 100,000 per day.

In the case of Alam, his career started as a failed businessman of tyre tube but flourished immensely as a successful business person of the export-oriented garment industry. For Kazi Aman, another entrepreneur, the starting journey was not the same. He began his career working in a buying house in 1992. While working in this buying house Aman had come into contact with some buyers over the years and developed a good relationship with them. He started to think about doing business with these buyers and shared his thoughts with two of his colleagues and they agreed to set up their own garment company. In 1996, they started to build a two-storey factory with an investment of Tk. 40,000. By the end of October 1998, the company started and contracts were made with buyers with whom they had previously communicated when they were in a buying house. They already knew about 10–15 such buyers, who had occasionally encouraged them to start a factory. Then, with two lines and about 200–250 workers, production started. But it was difficult for Aman to do business with partners. Splitting the profits and incurring profits was hard to gain in the company itself, unlike in a buying house. Moreover, there were differences of opinion as they thought differently when it came to strategies, and there were arguments too. Due to these anxieties, Aman broke his partnership and started his own garment company. After two decades of struggle, he is now sitting on the top floor of the corporate office building of his company in a factory which is no less than an estate, with multiple gates and a golf cart just to navigate the various facilities – this humble and modest beginning is nothing less than awe-inspiring.

3.2 Second-generation entrepreneurs

For the second-generation entrepreneurs, the garments sector is re-emerging as a lucrative sector in Bangladesh. It is one of the sectors where the capital gets multiplied within a very short span. Before entering this industry the general perception of the new generation about the garment industry was very sceptical – a small factory with unhealthy working conditions, less educated owner class with a traditional mindset, and workers protesting of their poor wages. Engaging in this industry might be the last thing the second generation would do. A corporate career in MNC, private banks, or with the telecommunication sector is a better option than dealing with the workers on the factory floor. The majority of the Bangladeshi youth do not know about the reality of this sector and only emphasize the negative sides as outsiders. This perspective has changed since new entrepreneurs – children of the owners – have started working in the garment factory voluntarily and in some cases involuntarily. Some of them wanted to expand the business of their parents but some did not have any choice. Against their will, they entered this industry instead of being a lawyer or settled overseas after graduation. Most of them started from an absolute zero idea and then gradually moved with a concrete plan. Since they have seen the garments sector from outsiders' perspective they have better absorption about the shifts in this sector on the ground. The story of two female entrepreneurs can be cited here.

Vidiya Amrit Khan is currently the Director of Desh Group of Companies, the first export-oriented garment company in Bangladesh. The legacy of her directorship was passed by her father, the late M. Noorul Quader, known as the pioneer of the garments industry in Bangladesh. Vidiya graduated as a qualified Barrister-at-law from King's College London, the U.K. in 2004. Her initial dream was to provide legal services to vulnerable people. However, reality diverted her to continue her father's legacy out of sheer love, passion, gratitude, and thankfulness. While growing up, she understood the endowment and history of this industry. Desh had to go through a lot of ups and downs. Her father died in 1998, and his departure, along with the natural calamity of the storm that severely damaged the factory in Chattogram, ultimately forced her to shut down for a few years. It created a requisite for Vidiya to undertake all the responsibilities and finally came back to Bangladesh from London to take charge of Desh in 2008. It was a challenging decision for her because all her life she had lived in London, in a very different social condition, and all of a sudden she had to move to a completely different set-up. She hired a German consultant to review the factory and according to his advice Vidiya, for the next four years, closely monitored the factory. During this period, she changed her daily routine and trained herself completely. In the factory, she got rid of all the inefficient workers, altered the production system, improved buyer–client relationships and brought highly coherent industrial engineers, and so on. Furthermore, she took on the job as the marketing director without any title and managed everything on her own. After a mature stand in the industry, Vidiya became one of the Directors of BGMEA with 27 male directors.

Another woman entrepreneur as well as Co-founder of Hay Festival in Dhaka, Sadaf never thought to start her career in garments. Born in New Jersey, she grew up in the U.K. and when she was 16, her family moved back to Bangladesh. It was a cultural shock for Sadaf to becoming a Bangladeshi. After finishing high school, she was desperate to go back to the U.K. and gained admission to the University of Cambridge to study Molecular Biology aiming for a research career in the future. However, while Sadaf was in Bangladesh, she was devastated by the poor social status of women in the country and felt it necessary to do something concrete to change the socio-cultural condition of the Bangladeshi women. Upon graduation, she did not follow the path of her peers; rather than stay on in the U.K. Sadaf returned to Bangladesh with her terms. Therefore, she decided to work for the development of women's overall condition in Bangladesh and joined "*Nari-Pokkho*" – a women development centric group. Meanwhile, she got married to someone having a similar interest. Her husband joined his family business to help his father who started a company named SITCO in 1984. One of the key business interests of SITCO was export-oriented garments. The company faced a huge loss when a buyer rejected a shipment for a reason SITCO was not responsible for. During this crisis, Sadaf joined the company for one year to re-build up the family business. After taking over the responsibility, Sadaf realized that the garment industry is the platform on which to engage actively in her desire for women empowerment since most of the workers in her factory are women. At the same time, there was an opportunity to showcase the garment industry of a Third World country positively and change the image of the country to the global market. To fulfil this mission, Sadaf launched her career as a garment entrepreneur.[4] According to Sadaf:

> Business people or people in business often didn't give business a good reputation. I believed, and still do, that business could be done in the right way and be successful. I remember a lot of people I knew looked down at the fact that I was getting involved in doing business.[5]

First-generation owners had to work very hard to find buyers, worry about compliance, source the fabrics, educate the workers in their ways, and work with people who were less versed in computer technology and machinery. In contrast, under the second-generation management, factories are well established with a solid plan, professional human resources, systematic and automated operation (see Box 3.1). The first generation has developed the industry in such a promising way that the buyers have become pursued to set up their local offices in Bangladesh. The most difficult job of getting the attention of the western buyers to this impoverished country has been done by the first generation and now it is up to the second generation to sustain and expand the industry with advanced technology and capitalist endeavour. The changes in the ownership structure of the Bangladesh RMG have been studied by the Centre for Policy Dialogue (CPD), a leading think-tank of the country, in 2019. The study explores that 65% of the garment companies are family-based private limited companies with the substantive role played by second-generation family members. About 88% of companies have on average three directors two of whom are from the same family. As the sector advances, the role of groups of companies in the RMG sector is becoming prominent. These groups encompass subsidiaries of both RMG and non-RMG enterprises of different categories. Another interesting finding of the study is the increasing tendency of the factories to move towards corporate practices. In the new working environment, increasing levels of delegation of authority are being shifted to the management who are educated and experienced. The research predicts, "With the rise in family businesses as well as increasing presence of second-generation family members in the businesses, the management structure is likely to be more corporatized in the coming years."

Such a prediction is not exaggerated. Compared to the garment entrepreneurs of the 1980s, the garment owners of the twenty-first century possess a unique vision – business sustainability. While the sector's growth remains healthy, there has been a serious concern over the failure to maintain a global labour standard. Especially after the Rana Plaza tragedy, the future of the Bangladesh RMG was under threat. The sustained failure of the government, as well as the management to address workplace safety, was exposed by the Rana Plaza disaster in 2013, in which more than 1,100 workers were killed. The tragedy triggered the emergence of two transnational governance approaches – Accord and Alliance initiated by the buyers and unions – and a government approach known as the National Initiative. The uniqueness of these initiatives is different key stakeholders worked together to address fire, electrical, and structural safety of factory buildings in a transparent and accountable way for the first time. The only option to be sustainable in the global supply chain is to ensure a global labour standard as prescribed by these initiatives. Unlike the traditional entrepreneurs, instead of buying extra assets such as land for the sake of 'safe investment', the second-generation entrepreneurs have intended to provide all the facilities as per the global regulations. They are proud of their factories for being compliant, employee-centric, worker-friendly, and equipped with modern technologies, and for bringing additional value to the workers by introducing different initiatives. To them, Rana Plaza was a blessing in disguise. According to a second-generation garment owner,

> Accord and Alliance is a brilliant step for Bangladesh that has happened after the Rana Plaza incident. The other non-garment industries should have similar systems like that. The basic problems are being mitigated and there is no place for institutional discrepancies anymore. Although the profit margin has decreased compared to the past years but the working environment has changed significantly, it costs three times more money to start a business now. Workers have better pay ranges, improved facilities and permanency in jobs. There are compliances to ensure a safer environment for the workers and every factory has to abide by the rules otherwise they will not receive a certificate from the Accord and Alliance and the orders will automatically get discarded. Factories have their engineers to supervise and ensure building safety. Now foreign orders are chasing our industries because of skilled labor and other comparative advantages, we are no longer struggling to compete. Bangladesh should have a third party interference than having its government to intervene. Our focus should be making Accord and Alliance more accommodating for us. They are saving our garment industry owners and opening ways to comprehend business.

The industry is very confident about the second generation of the garments sector. Now it has skilled workers, safe investments, better managerial systems, and modern types of machinery. The new generation adds newer philosophies to improve the industry. Hence, time is changing, workers are not suffering like in the 1980s, and their necessities are ensured. There is a culture to establish a good relationship with buyers. The garment owners no longer need the government to penetrate the market; they can search on their own, and this freedom is bringing positive connotation to the future marketplace in Bangladesh.

How optimistic the first-generation owners are to the second generation – that is a valid question since not all of them have opted for this profession voluntarily. Let's find it out from the observation of four first-generation owners mentioned earlier in this chapter. There is no doubt that Bangladesh RMG is still a competitive industry and will flourish in the future. If the current management performs properly through hard work in this sector, there is still a lot of business here. The older generation did not learn the business by studying; rather their knowledge of doing business was through day-to-day practical experiences in the factory. The second generation is much more educated and absorbs rational and practical behaviour. From his own experiences, Alam, a first-generation owner, feels confident to hand over greater responsibility of the factory to his son in the future. His son comes to the factory two days a week and teaches at a leading private university for the remaining days of the week. Alam gave an assignment to his son to impart some practical knowledge as he expects his son to eventually take over the business alongside his other pursuits. The assignment was to deal with a Russian buyer who came to Bangladesh to do business. It turns out that as Alam mentioned, the buyer was so impressed with the presentation and hospitality of his son that confirmed the deal before leaving the country. According to Alam, "Even the Merchandiser, who was trained and experienced in his factory, expressed that the way Alam's son had handled the report, explained the services of the company, understood the requirements of the buyers, was excellent and very efficient." Thus, the new generation is expected to bring about a lot of changes, and increase productivity, and this will possibly gear up the industry towards attaining a higher market share in the future. Alam is optimistic about the capacity of the second generation to do much better than the previous generation in the market.

However, Aman and Das are not as optimistic as Alam. From their experiences, they feel that the younger generation does not want to work for long hours as they did. To them, the second generation will work hard, but for a shorter time. They dislike the idea of working for long hours or travelling a long time for the job. "I've been coming to Narayanganj from Gulshan for the past 30 years" – sharing this five hours daily travel from home to factory Aman thinks such dedication is missing in the young generation. Because of the shorter work habit of his son, Aman's company is expanding towards the spinning mills as those can be managed by the younger generation. The spinning mill requires less one to one human contact that is necessary for the factory level. Such less pressure on work will release some time for his son to maintain a more relaxed lifestyle. Das agrees with Aman on the lack of dedication of the second generation to take more responsibility in the business. Das pushes his son to take control of the company and deal with the staff from the office to the factory. He wishes his song will take charge more and become more active in the business. He has sent his son to the best schools and provided him with an excellent education, the best he could afford, which has taken a lot of hard work; he expects the same of his son, who, as Das stated, is still unwary of the hardships his father had to face to establish this business. Both Das and Aman argue that the RMG is a buyer-driven industry and the nature of work does not allow a 9–5 office time; it requires long hours' engagement. The second generation should find pleasure in the job that will pursue them to step up in taking greater responsibility and commitment to work as long as it is required. Also, the long hours will pay off, and to achieve something one must put in an effort.

Box 3.1 Transforming traditions: Ananta Group

Challenging traditional norms and innovating to push boundaries have been the guiding principles that have propelled Ananta Group into becoming one of Bangladesh's most prominent garment manufacturers. The organization was established in 1991 by Humayun Zahir. The initial years of Ananta Group saw it venture into manufacturing industries such as garments, paper mills, and toys. The sons, Sharif Zahir and Asif Zahir had to take over Ananta Group after their father's demise. After taking over, the brothers revamped the organization and went on to make a mark in the highly competitive garments industry in Bangladesh. "I believe in stability; we were young at the time and wanted to change everything, so I took time to adjust," said Sharif. Having been driven by the values set by their father, as well as learning from big industry players, Sharif and Asif Zahir set out to differentiate themselves in an already established industry. They led the group in a new direction, focussing on specializing in the garments industry and initiating an industry-wise transformation. When they started, Ananta Group consisted of a single factory with 1,500 employees, but through their efforts at expansion, the organization, as of 2018, consists of eight factories with 26,000 employees. A defining characteristic of Ananta Group has been its tendency to break out of the mould for Bangladesh's garments industry. As Bangladesh is well known for denim bottoms, Ananta Group initially focussed on the value-added aspect of the product, developing expertise in the finishing process. Additionally, the organization has not been afraid to venture into a diversified range of products within the apparel industry that are not common in Bangladesh, such as suits, sweaters and lingerie, thus making it both unique and a pioneer. Ananta grew at rates of 25–30% per year in the last decade, while the industry grew at 15–20%, thereby staying well ahead of the curve. The driving force behind Ananta Group's growth has been the shared passion of the brothers to make a difference. "We were quite obsessed...I was quite obsessed with what I was doing. Our discussion from morning till evening at home, all our private discussions, were about the company. Even now it's like that," said Sharif. Asif, after his stint with Google, joined his elder brother Sharif at the FB and complemented him in terms of strategic thinking. They focussed heavily on bringing in the best talent to help create a proper management structure. They recruited talent not only from the local market but also from overseas. "We want to bring global best practices to Bangladesh. We bring in talent and international exposure to help develop and innovate each sector we are in," said Asif. The recruitment of highly skilled employees and trusted delegation of operations have allowed Ananta Group to create an atmosphere of shared passion, loyalty and excitement amongst everyone in the organization. This atmosphere is credited to the group's rapid growth. The group's values also prioritize environmental and social impacts in what it does. The organization has focussed on ensuring that its factories received international certifications and that energy-conserving technologies have been installed within its operations. In addition to that, Ananta Group has reached out to communities that its employees belong to by working with one of the largest NGOs in the world on initiatives such as improving hygiene within communities, supporting hospitals, and improving worker training and education.

> We never want to be a small player in any industry we enter. There will always be opportunities elsewhere, but we have to be careful with how we diversify. We have specific competencies that will allow us to be successful,

said Asif. The brothers are already disrupting the real estate and e-commerce industries. They believe their values, ability to attract talent, and strategic approach will lead them to become leaders in any new industries they may enter.

(Case study from PwC Bangladesh Family Business Survey, 2018).

3.3 Sources of power

One of the unique characteristics of the garment owners regardless of different generations is exercising a large degree of influence over the government because of their close association with the political elite and ruling parties of Bangladesh. The owners' association, i.e. BGMEA and BKMEA (Bangladesh Knitwear Manufacturers and Exporters Association), are the platforms for exercising this power. In the parliament, for example, almost 10% of the MPs (Member of Parliament) are directly involved in the garments industry (Labowitz and Bauman-Pauly, 2014). Businessmen have been dominating the parliament in recent years. In 1973 only 13% of businessmen were elected in parliament elections, while by 2008 a major 63% were businessmen. The association of businessmen and politicians or as a matter of fact, the combination of both has become a means of capturing state power. Within this framework, access to capital and resources allows further consolidation of political power. For instance, the current Commerce Minister of Bangladesh was the president of BGMEA and owner of a garment company, the current Mayor of Dhaka North city corporation was the president of BGMEA in 2013–2014 as well as a garment entrepreneur, the former Mayor of Dhaka North city corporation, the late Annisul Huq, was the president of BGMEA in 2005 and a garment owner.

The nature of state can explain the state-business nexus in Bangladesh. The Bangladesh state has been criticized for being a weak state, whose weakness has its roots in the colonial period. One of the reasons for the existence of a weak state in Bangladesh is the absence of democratic culture and political commitment within the major political parties (Zafarullah, 2003). The absence of a democratic culture causes the governments not to pursue strong state policies. The government remains dependent on the economic elite class.

> This reflects a general pattern in Third World states whereby, according to Chaplan, 'the state as a simple agency for extraction and control' is the ultimate 'prize in political competition, and [is] a means by which those who win that competition can serve their ambitions and suppress their opponents'.
>
> (Zafarullah, 2003: 288)

Close ties exist between the government – both military and democratic – and the businesspeople. the state-owned enterprises (SOEs) were sold most for give-away prices in the 1980s to the business class without determining the value of an SOE in the market, and subsidized credits were given to the entrepreneurs and created an environment in which the business sector could abuse its power (Palmer, 1994; Quadir, 2000). The military rulers practised government patronage by favouring the business elites and this has been done to legitimize their power. But the tendency of establishing close ties with the business elites has continued under democratic governments since 1991. For instance, the government awarded more than 30 quick rental power plant to private companies who were directly or indirectly related to the ruling political party (Mirza, 2019). One of the factors that contribute to this process is not to legitimize politicians' power but to meet the costs of elections and to generate party funds. Kibria, the former Finance Minister, has stated that one of the factors in ensuring election victory is to gain the ability to spend millions of dollars during the election (The Daily Star, 1994). The close ties between government and business have resulted in significant loan defaults as a result of government patronage. For instance, the volume of loan defaults in the four National Commercial Banks rose by 29% or Tk. 2,885 crore during December 2005–March 2006 and the loan defaults of Private Commercial Banks was Tk. 3,796 crore (The Daily Star, 2006). As of December 2019, according to Bangladesh Bank, the amount of loan default increased to Tk. 10,11,828 crore, the highest in South Asia (New Age, 2020). Under the protection of the ruling party, the business elites have refused to return the loans they have taken from various financial institutions. Nevertheless, the position of businessmen in politics violates a few laws, especially in parliament. An MP having personal interests in the sector that he/she is involved in cannot be in the standing committee of that sector in parliament. This is outlined by the rules of procedure (RoP) of the Bangladesh parliament. As stated in section 188, "No member shall be appointed to a Committee who has a personal, pecuniary or direct interest in any matter which may be considered by that Committee" (Representation of the People Act, 2013). Other MPs are indirectly involved in having interests or having associates or family members within the industry. It has been observed that BGMEA's internal leadership changes correspond to changes in the national ruling party. No matter which political party is in power, individuals connected with the political party belong in the spotlight and can exert influence within the BGMEA leadership.

Many questions were raised though about BGMEA's authority and regulatory power. An export clearance, known as Utilization Declaration (UD) is done by BGMEA, which is usually issued by state agencies for other industries. For example, in the pharmaceutical industry in Bangladesh, export clearances are done through the Department of Narcotics Control and require applications to get permission. This ability to have UD clearance is essential in the sense that it endows permission to a factory to import or export. This begs the question, of how much authority a business organization should have in a country, which is legally not a regulatory entity (TIB, 2013).

Factories closely associated with the leadership rarely face penalties for compliance issues. In 2010, a factory owned by Hameem Group caught fire and killed more than 26 people (The Daily Star, 2010). The managing director AK Azad was also the president of FBCCI then. At the time of the incident, the factory was said to be producing high-level retail such as Gap. The Clean Clothes Campaign has frequently contacted the Hameem Group about "violations of freedom of association and other labour standards at the company's factories". At the same time, eyewitnesses mentioned that at least two of the six exits were locked and this was a common occurrence for the building (Clean Clothes Campaign, 2010). Despite these violations, the factory has never responded to these issues until the accident. BGMEA has compensated the families of victims by giving them 100,000 taka each, while the injured would get 25,000 taka each. Despite the accident, Azad was focussed on orders as quoted "There might be some problems in meeting buyer orders (The Daily Star, 2010) – instead of safety and compliance."

The press releases on BGMEA's official website as well as general news report also highly identify the strong links between the two press releases from BGMEA's website: "BGMEA hails Govt decision on army called in at Ctg Port," or "BGMEA hails govt decision on fertilizer factories to save gas," (BGMEA, 2016), strongly imply the rooting of BGMEA's leadership for stronger association and times with the government. It could even be argued that BGMEA, rather than being a neutral institution working in favour of the garments; it is an extension of the government's as well as industry's interests in keeping the garments industry in the most profitable shape possible.

A recent example of similar interests is highlighted by BGMEA and the government's response to a TIB Report titled "Undress Corruption" released in the first month of January, which uncovers corruption within the industry. The report indicated compliance bribes, suppliers influencing a purchase decision, violation of minimum wage/labour rights, illegal subcontracting to save money, bribe offered to audit, etc. Within the period of a few days, BGMEA did a press release, in which BGMEA president Siddiqur Rahman stated "The timing of the TIB Report is thus against the interest of the country's garment industry, as it questions the integrity of the stakeholders along with world-class third party auditors and clients" as well as calling the report "baseless, intentional, mischievous and far from the truth" (The Daily Star, 2016). Almost immediately following BGMEA's press release, former Commerce Minister Tofail Ahmed commented that a case should be filed against TIB for "false, motivated and imaginary reports on the readymade garment industry," in a similar vein commenting on how the report is carrying out a motivated and intentional campaign to hurt the industry. The almost unanimous response showcases how the garment owners exercise power and BGMEA along with the government operate almost on a similar level – further consolidating the fact that their interests and stake in the industry coincide.[6]

Another example of RMG owners' political power is the establishment of RMG Sustainability Council (RSC). As mentioned above three inspection governance systems were introduced after the Rana Plaza to ensure factory building safety – Accord, Alliance, and National Initiative. The first two were governed by the transnational agency and the last one by the government's DIFE (Department of Inspection for Factories and Establishments). The Alliance ceased its operation in 2018 and Accord in 2020 after a two-year extension of the original agreement in 2018. There had been a great concern over the replacement of Accord. In principle, it was expected that the DIFE would take over the inspection authority of all garment factories. Although, in the past, there was a question of the capacity of this government's department, after the tragedy the government of Bangladesh has made several major commitments to revamp DIFE. The number of inspectors has been increased from 183 pre-Rana Plaza to 575 post-Rana Plaza, and the budget was increased from $0.97 million before 2013 to $4.1 million in 2015–2016 (Shipar, 2017). Different national and international organizations, along with the development partners, have extended their support to build up the capacity of the government. A Remediation Coordination Cell (RCC) has been formed to manage the remediation work of the factories inspected by the NI supported by ILO with funding from Canada, the U.K., and the Netherlands. Because of these rapid and effective changes, the DIFE was the right regulatory authority to take over the Accord. Surprisingly, BGMEA took the initiative to establish RSC, a private multi-stakeholder regulatory body led by the garment owners' association. The RSC has taken over all Accord Bangladesh operations which will be governed by representatives of the BGMEA, global brands, and global and national trade unions. It will be operating under the legal framework of the government of Bangladesh and in close cooperation with the Ministry of Commerce and collaboration with the Ministry of Labor and Employment and DIFE (BGMEA, 2020). The formation of RSC shows the extent of political power the garment owners exercise in the country by undermining the authority of a public regulatory system. At the same time, the weaker and vulnerable position of a state creates a space for a private regulatory body. After 49 years of independence, still, the local and global actors do not have the confidence to rely on the public regulatory institution of the country.

Even so, a small glimpse of hope is evident in the state's demolishing of the BGMEA's headquater, a 15-storeyed tower deemed to be built illegally. The Bangladesh High Court notified that not only was the land illegally obtained, but the tower was also built without proper authorization and blocked drainage systems (New York Times, 2013). The building complex also took up additional space not mentioned in earlier plans. Even the Dhaka city development authority RAJUK, objected to building this office in the part of the land (The Daily Star, 2019). While the court gave 90 days for it to be demolished, the building stood in a symbolic gesture of how powerful the organization is. When asked about the legitimacy of the building, the late Annisul Huq, former President of BGMEA, said, "It is not illegal...we have applied to the government for the land. The government has given us the land. Two prime ministers have opened it. What validation do you want?" (New York Times, 2013). The statement holds though – Prime minister Sheikh Hasina laid the foundation for the building in 1998, and Khaleda Zia, former Prime Minister held the inauguration of the building in 2006. The High Court issued the order to tear down the building in 2011 and finally the authority has started to demolish the building in 2020.

Notes

1 Interview with the researcher on December 10, 2003.
2 Out of these four entrepreneurs, one was interviewed in 2003–2004 as part of my doctoral dissertation and three from one of my research projects conducted in 2016–2018.
3 Interview with the author, January 14, 2004, Dhaka, Bangladesh.
4 Sadaf is placed in this study as a second-generation entrepreneur because of her similarities to other second generation owners in this book.
5 In an interview and email communication with Sadaf on September 22, 2020.
6 https://www.hrw.org/news/2013/12/15/bangladesh-companies-fail-compensate-firevictims.

4 Case study

Small garment factory

4.1 Rise and demise of a compliant factory

Bantai was a Bangladeshi company that manufactured sportswear at its factory in Kalyanpur, Dhaka, from 1990 to 2005. There are two key reasons for conducting a case study of this company. First, the way a small garment company started up was different from other Bangladeshi garment companies. The company believed that the basic rights of workers for a safe and healthy work environment are as important as corporate productivity and profitability. The management team also believed businesses should take responsibility for providing social services for workers, such as family planning, education for children, and day care. All these features made the company special and unique. Second, the closure of its operation showed the company's fatal vulnerability after almost a decade of prosperous growth. Bantai was a joint-venture company with a Taiwanese partner. Each partner was exclusively signed to their respective roles: the agreement was that the Bangladeshi partner of Bantai would be in charge of production and the Taiwanese partner would manage the marketing role. But the success of this company was fatally undermined by the departure of a Taiwanese partner from Bantai.

Bantai started its business with 350 workers in 1990 and the number had increased to 460 in 2000. Most of the workers in Bantai migrated to the cities from rural areas. About 90% of the workforce was female, the average age was 25 years, and almost half were married. Bantai operated its business from a factory of 26,000 square feet in size located in Dhaka, housed the offices of the MD, GM, and finance manager, as well as 360 machines producing sportswear.

The workplace was also relatively safe and healthy compared to other Bangladeshi garment factories in the 1990s. The shift regularly began at 7.30 a.m. and finished at 4.30 p.m. including a 1-hour lunch break. The workers could take a break to pray at lunch. The most important feature of Bantai was that the workers received a fixed salary. In general, the salary package was quite standard as per the labour law before 2006 – monthly salary Taka (Tk.) 1,200, house rent Tk. 360, medical Tk. 150, presence bonus Tk. 50, and production bonus Tk. 150. For overtime, the workers received double payment (e.g. if an employee worked 2 hours, they received payment of 4 hours). Whereas most garment workers in other factories did not receive their salary on time, Bantai workers were fortunate. Tara, a Bantai employee, stated, "We get our salary timely which is very important for us."[1] Landlords preferred to rent homes to Bantai workers because they received their salaries on time. Due to regular payment of salary, employees were loyal to the company and it was expressed by the following statement of the MD:

> One day I went to the floor and found one worker was sick and eyes looked red. I told the supervisor to let her leave. But the worker didn't want to leave. She told me that we have a shipment today and two workers in her section were absent. So she will work on the shipment. They consider it's their factory, own product.[2]

The factory operated six days per week. During major festivals, such as Eid (a Muslim religious festival), the factory remained closed for seven days, though the holiday only lasts three days. Two bonuses (i.e. half of the salary) were available for Bantai employees for two major festivals in a year. Compared to other factories, Bantai was exceptional. For example, there was no night shift for workers. During work time, music is played constantly as a way to entertain the workers and alleviate their stress.

The company reacted sympathetically during hard times for their workers and assisted when there were personal crises. For example, Aleya, a 35-year-old employee, took leave for seven days in 1998. But because her brother had died during that time, she felt she could not return to work at the end of her leave. She was therefore allowed to extend her leave. Bantai did not cut her salary because she took additional leave. Rina, another worker, received maternity leave for three months including salary and maternity leave allowance. This is unusual in the Bangladesh garment industry. If the workers were unable to work because of a factory accident, Bantai paid wages for the downtime.

Management has also stated that it wanted to ensure that supervisors did not abuse the workers. If workers made errors, supervisors were told to try their best to make the workers understand what went wrong. If any supervisor misbehaved with workers, management took strong action against the supervisor. The factory had one supervisor per section of the factory and female supervisors for female workers. Cutting, which is a male-dominated craft in most parts of the world, had a male supervisor. Fieldwork interviews indicated that employees and supervisors seemed to understand each other. Workers typically expressed their feelings in the following way:

> After working many days together we are very close to each other and feel like a family. Here everyone is like brother and sister. A supervisor behaves like a sister. If any worker has any kind of problem during

> the working time, the supervisor comes forward to solve it - suppose give some rest, take a break. Sometimes the next worker does the job of the worker who is on a break. If anyone is sick, the supervisor allows leaving.[3]

Bantai implemented welfare programmes in the workplace. Mr. Rahman's management ideology was structured around the core notion that if employees were well-treated they were likely to be dedicated. The welfare programmes included a health project, family planning, a crèche, an education centre for the workers' children, a saving scheme, a fair-priced shop, and entertainment programmes. Recruits to Bantai were provided with a health card on which their detailed health history was recorded. All the workers were trained about basic health and hygiene through discussions and posters. Bantai first introduced a health programme with the co-operation of Dhaka Community Hospital whose mission is to help the poor. A female doctor from Dhaka Community Hospital, who was retained on contract by Bantai, visited the factory at least once a week and provided the treatment, advice, and guidance required by the workers. On other working days, when the doctor was not available in the factory, patients could meet the doctor in the hospital. Pathological tests, consultation with specialist doctors, secondary and tertiary medical services (including hospitalization, major surgical operations, etc.) were all carried out at the hospital and paid for by Bantai. Basic awareness, advice, and guidance about family planning were provided to the Bantai workers by a professional NGO called Concerned Women for Family Planning. They provided contraceptives (e.g. pills, condoms, and injections) to the workers during monthly visits to the factory. Minor clinical services, if required, were also provided at the premises, while patients were referred to the NGO's base clinic for major clinical or surgical problems.

Bantai established day care facilities within its factory premises. Complete care was provided to the babies throughout the day by professionally trained ayas (nannies). They participated in a preventive health care programme, e.g. immunization and vaccination on entry, and the children were given balanced food at least three times a day. The workers could see their children during work and feed them. The workers said they were very satisfied with this care, and for this reason, they could concentrate on their work. Hajera Begum, for example, stated that one of the reasons for joining Bantai was the day-care service. She had felt worried about leaving her child at home. Now she could work without any fear. Another worker, Baby said:

> My husband is a rickshaw rider. I also want to earn money for the family. I have three children. For my children, I could not work. There was no one to take care of my children. For this reason, it was very tough to work. I heard about Bantai 11 years ago, where there is a daycare centre. I joined Bantai due to the service of daycare. My three children [were] brought up in this centre for four years. After that, they got admission

> to Bantai School. When they were in daycare, I looked after my children during working time. In this case, the supervisor was generous and considerate.

Bantai ran a small school in the factory. Trained teachers, paid by the company, worked with 90 students in two shifts of primary education. Graduates from the school could enrol in grade five in public school after four years with Bantai. The students were provided with free tuition, books, stationery, snacks, and entertainment facilities. The school was not only an institution that provided proper education to the children but also a place to take care of them while their mothers are at work. The children had the chance to grow in a proper environment for their balanced development. At the same time, the mothers became aware of the need to educate their children.

In a male-dominated society like Bangladesh, money earned by women is controlled by male members of the family – usually the husband. Hence, most of the workers at Bantai did not initially reveal their actual income to members of their families. Approximately 20% of their monthly wages were invested in one or more of the following savings schemes: (1) Accounts in a nationalized bank near the factory; (2) Deposit pension scheme in the post office and nationalized bank; (3) Informal savings groups within different work sections of the factory. Through these schemes, workers became aware of the potential scope for social and economic development through savings. They had cash, which enhanced their decision-making position in the family, and could use it for buying assets and property. Another very important aspect of this scheme was that this disadvantaged group was introduced to the formal financial institutions and could escape the grip of the traditional money-lenders and users, who operated their businesses at exorbitant rates of interest – sometimes more than 10% per month. Bantai's GM stated:

> Each worker has a bank account and the management take care of the account. The workers don't know how to do banking. In this regard, the management sometimes fills up their forms and help them. It is hard for a banker to manage all the workers who are small customers but we maintain good relations with the bank. We also have an account record in our factory of the workers. So the workers can know their current account from us.

The welfare and development programmes operated for the Bantai workers had very positive impacts on both the workforce and the finance of the company as a whole. Bantai started welfare activities without thinking of financial benefits as argued by the MD of the company. It was, however, found that welfare programmes had a positive impact on profitability. The worker turnover rate was one of the lowest until 2001 – at which time the Taiwanese partner left the company. In terms of absenteeism rates, employees had been with Bantai on average for eight years which is significant. The workers had a sense of full participation, ownership, and unquestionable loyalty to the company. From the time of its formation, there had never been any strike, unrest, or agitation in the company. The important thing to note is that the company had a happy workforce, which affected output insofar as workers could concentrate more on their jobs and produce fewer errors. The rate of rejection (i.e. the number of finished products rejected by buyers due to low quality and faulty products) was 0.1% whereas in the garment trade the average rate of rejection is 1.5%. It may appear at first glance that the cost of managing welfare programmes would be excessive. But the Bantai experience indicates that its welfare programme cost approximately 1% of the total production cost as stated by the GM of Bantai. The General Manager of the company expressed these views:

> The workers trust us. They believe what we say to them. We don't take any unnecessary steps. Sometimes we have an order problem. Then we may not take care of 100% of them. They show sympathy in this matter. When [it] is happening in the business, they know that. If we are making a profit they are happy, if we lose the market they feel sorry. Some factories in Bangladesh make a profit but don't pay salaries to the workers. They tell them they are not profiting which is not true. We don't do this. That's why we are trustworthy to the workers. Sometimes we need more workers if we get a big order. Last month we needed some operators and advertise for workers. Within a week we got the workers. If the workers hear that Bantai needs workers they immediately contact us. Even they come to us leaving another job. It happens because of our good reputation.

One of the reasons for this kind of loyalty was the welfare programmes. They had a direct impact on production, increasing productivity and improving the products. The monthly production of the company for sportswear was 40,000 dozen in 1991 and rose to 50,000 dozen in 2000 Putting social development programmes in place not only satisfied Bangladesh's legal requirements and complied with corporate responsibilities but also met the social and moral obligations of the company's owner. At the same time, the owner of Bantai felt satisfied with the effectiveness of different social programmes. According to Mr. Rahman,

> You can find a difference between my garment workers and others. What we are trying to [get them to] understand that they can build up [their] own future from the position they have. They need to be confident, conscious about rights. That's why my garment workers do not give dowry.

Now, what is significant in a broader context is how industrial society reacted to Bantai's ideology of implementing welfare programmes. In 1993,

100 garment entrepreneurs attended a seminar organized by the Islami Bank where Mr. Rahman had a chance to talk for 15 minutes on the subject of doing business with social welfare. But he could not speak for more than 4 minutes before he was asked to shut up because Mr. Rahman was stating that it is a decent and moral duty for employers to take a proactive role towards their workers. The lesson Mr. Rahman learned from the meeting was that his approach was wrong. Two years after that meeting, the media focused on Bantai's welfare programmes. It was telecast on national TV. In an interview, Mr. Rahman did not make the same mistake. He discussed the economic benefits of good practice in the factory, which had a more effective result. Mr. Rahman stated:

> Now I tell the garment employers that your attitude should be right. Big buyers have codes of conduct. Despite that, workers are not empowered. Why? I am forced. I am doing it without my conscience. I am doing it without my involvement. For that reason, the workers are not getting the impact. Why people are poor in my country — because they are not confident. Workers have a lack of confidence. The British destroyed our confidence. Poor people have no pride, no dream. If you want to give these, you can't do it only by offering welfare. You need to convince them that it is your job and it is my job. There is no difference between you and me. In this way, they can raise their head.[4]

Bantai developed relations of reciprocity with its workers. On the one hand, management offered welfare programmes to empower employees and, on the other hand, workers invested their energy and showed complete commitment for the sake of company profitability. This cycle continued effectively for eleven years until the foreign partner left the company in 2001. The reason for the partner's departure was that the Taiwanese partner chose China as a better investment opportunity compared to Bangladesh. Suddenly Bantai found it very difficult to get the order from the buyer. After 2001, orders began to decrease drastically. The number of workers at Bantai had decreased from 480 to 150 as the company could not afford them. Sometimes the workers had no work as there was no order or no load. Consequently, employees began to worry about their future. Although they received a monthly salary, whether there was work or not, employees did not want to receive money in this way. They wanted to work hard for Bantai and expected regular buying orders. Moni, a garment worker, stated, "We want that our employer makes progress in the business. We want to say that we are right behind him. We pray that the employer gets regular orders from the buyers." Another worker, Taslima, also felt the same way:

> Whenever an order comes we work here with our hearts as not to make any mistakes. Many buyers, in the past, were pleased with our service and we got orders. But now we don't get regular orders. It makes us feel very bad.

Bantai's MD expressed his concern about the decline of the company:

> Now what you are watching is that the company is dying. When the Taiwanese partner left us we are down in business. Now the worker size is 150. Others left, as there is no work. My colleagues are trying to get the order. If we can't survive we will close it down.

Ultimately Bantai was forced to close its operation in 2005 – all the workers lost their jobs and a responsible entrepreneur disappeared from the garment business. It had been a company that was considered a model for the rest of Bangladesh's garment companies. But it became vulnerable and failed to survive in the global market. The withdrawal of assistance from the foreign partner was one cause behind its collapse. But, from a broader perspective, this was the result of the momentous pressures of neoliberal globalization.

The advent of Bantai initiated opportunities for women workers to exercise greater independence and to provide a better life for themselves and their families. For example, Shahida, 25 years of age, had been working at Bantai for five years. She had one daughter who attended Class One at Bantai School. Before joining Bantai, Shahida lived in her village as a housewife. Later, she migrated to Dhaka where her husband worked in a grocery shop. In the city, Shahida found that the cost of living was very high. She attended to the task of helping her husband in managing the daily costs. All through her life, she did not work outside the home due to social norms but later she wanted to earn money. Shahida was able to pay the house rent from her salary. She rightly felt that she was trying to do something for her family. Another worker, 30-year-old Shomita, joined Bantai in 1994. After working for three years, she left the job due to marriage. She went to her village where she looked after her parents. Her husband was a sanitary worker who lives in the city. Shomita has two children. The family's expenditure had increased. Shomita also had a major operation which cost $200. All these costs put pressure on her family. Shomita decided to earn some money for the family and re-joined Bantai in 2002. The closure of Bantai has shattered the dreams of Shahida and Shomita. These are the workers who broke the bonds of orthodox society and wanted to share the responsibility of their families and become independent, but their future dreams are now under threat.

The workers who lost their jobs may be able to obtain jobs in other garment factories but their working conditions might not be as developed as they were in Bantai. One group of employees worked at another garment factory before their employment at Bantai and became interested in joining Bantai for its reputation as a safe workplace. For example, Bokul, a garment worker at Bantai, worked there for twelve years. Before working in Bantai, she worked in a different factory for three years. But she experienced several problems there. Due to working the night shift, she did not come home until after 10 p.m. Another problem was an irregular salary. Sometimes she didn't get paid for overtime. For these reasons, she left her previous place of employment and joined Bantai for better conditions. Another worker, Nurbanu, came from Vola (a district) where she was reading in Class Eight. She had six sisters and one brother. To visit her brother's home, she came to Dhaka five years ago. There she got married and could not return to the village but joined Bantai. Her husband allowed her to work there, as Bantai was a safe place for women. Bokul and Nurbanu will again search for jobs, and if they find employment, there is no certainty that they will work in a safe and secure workplace such as Bantai.

4.2 Struggles of a non-compliant factory

Shaon Das commenced export-oriented garment company "Texphin" with two partners.[5] There was a setback at the beginning. Disagreement with strategy forced a partner to leave the company with his initial investment of Tk. 14 lacs. Although Das was also not happy with another partner for lack of professionalism he has tried to adapt to the situation. The factory space was used for the marriage anniversary of a partner's son and lunch was offered from factory accounts. Anyway, Texphin produces simple t-shirts with white fabric. To keep up with the buyers' demand, the company tries to improve the technology. For instance, a buyer's requirement was that the t-shirts only have 5% shrinkage and very few fold marks. So, to address these issues the drying or dewatering machine used previously called hydro extractor was replaced with the new technology – squeezer machine available in Indonesia – costing about $31,000. The management knew that the British technology for these squeezers was of a better quality, but they purchased the Indonesian squeezers at a low price. Investments were also made in buying the Italian finishing machines to upgrade the quality of finishing. The profile of Texphin is presented in table 4.1.

Table 4.1 Profile of Texphin

Workers' profile	*Wage and OT (average)*	*Regulation*	*Labour organization*	*Management qualification*
Size 182	Wages 2013: Tk. 650,000	No third party audit	No WPC	Factory manager: Graduate
Turnover 21%	Wages 2017: Tk. 682,000	No buyers' code of conduct	No safety committee and union	Production manager: Diploma
Absenteeism 7%	OT 2013: 120,000			General manager: Diploma
Average tenure 1 year	OT 2017: 120,000			
	Monthly mini mum Tk. 5,300			

Source: Management survey (2017–2018).

The numbers of contract-based workers have seen a significant rise in successive years. The reason for the trend can be sighted as the increasing availability of jobs in various factories of the same industry. Salary and benefits tend to be the deciding factors in the decision-making of the transference of the labour force jobs. Initially, the factory was dominated by male workers, about 70%. Gradually though, the female workers had increased to 60% of the workforce. Because men are more outgoing, they tend to look for ways to avoid working, but women tend to be relatively dedicated to their jobs, focus more on their work. So women tend to have a better output at Texphin, especially since they have better concentration capability in knitting and sewing work. Another reason for recruiting female workers is less engagement in grouping and wreaking havoc in the workplace. However, considering the gender perspective, the more laborious tasks such as packaging and ironing are reserved for men, while women workers are mostly employed in sewing tasks. Quite surprisingly, the company appointed few women to mid-level management positions. Because a majority of women work in the production lines and sometimes it is required for the supervisors to show the workers how they should work. This requires physical contact, so having a female supervisor helps in that case. It was a lesson for the company. In the past, a female worker had filed a complaint against a production manager who was male. She was offended when the production manager had touched her arm to show how to operate the machinery to get the best result. The management found that the whole scenario occurred as part of group politics and the production manager was let off with a formal warning. In another case, a male operator was fired for several complaints by female workers. Providing misinformation to the union and owners' association, the operator tried to get back to his job but the top management of Texphin defended their decision.

Overall the factory was disorganized. The workers had punch cards but the punching machine was dysfunctional and workers were just signed in by hand for attendance. Sometimes the workers did not put the right timing, coming in late but signing at an earlier time. The owners' perception of workers is not promising. Das said:

> With no qualifications or proof of certification, there was no way to ensure that the workers are capable or skillful. The only assurance is a word of mouth recommendation that the workers have previously worked somewhere. Moreover, the workers have no commitment or loyalty to the companies they work for, so in many cases, it turns out that they leave the company in the middle of a job. Sometimes, the mid-level employees leave their job and take with them a chunk of the working population when moving to a new factory, and the company is left with a major loss in production and might even face a shipment failure which is a major blow to the reputation and incurs a massive loss for the company.

There are no training programmes for the workers to improve efficiency. The company had some bad experiences in the past regarding training employees. A young man upon the request of a friend was recruited and seeing his dedication to work, was sent to Taiwan for a paid training of three months. Upon returning, he told the owner he wanted to get married, and so he was given a further Tk. 10,000. However, he never returned to work. There are many such stories where, after receiving training, employees left the company as they could now attain better-paying jobs at other companies. All the investments in training waste in vain as stated by the management.

The major reason that workers leave the factory is that they do not have many options to receive overtime. The production manager says that amongst the 182 workers, of whom 70 are permanent with others being piece-rate workers or helpers, about 8–10 are always absent. This is because they hardly ever earn more than the fixed amount, that is, Tk. 5,200 for the permanent workers, and for the piece-rate workers a revenue that is determined based on their work. For example, if an operator is appointed to fix buttons at Tk. 3 per dozen and he manages to complete 500 such sets, he is paid Tk. 1,500. In bigger factories, which have a lot more orders, the workers can opt for working overtime, which by the end of the month turns their salary to about Tk. 9,000 or Tk. 10,000, so they want to work for a large or medium factory with overtime options.

Meanwhile, some problems arise with the piece-rate workers especially during a big order when there is pressure to complete an order within a short time. The production manager says that the machines have a knob to fix the number of stitches per inch (SPI), which is turned to a certain number by the supervisors before work begins, but it turns out that sometimes the workers tweak with the machines so that the SPI is decreased and the output of clothes is increased. This, in turn, affects the quality of the clothes and tends to make them unacceptable for the order, incurring losses for the factory.

The workers did not receive a salary before the middle of the month. Withholding the payment of workers until mid-month was a management strategy so that workers won't leave the factory at the beginning of the month. However, sometimes this strategy of delayed payment intentionally demotivate workers. Another reason for the late salary was a lack of consensus between partners. The workers expect payment to be made on a certain date, but other partners hold the money, so workers are disheartened when they do not get paid.

The workers were not allowed to form a union or WPC since this might lead to labour unrest. The management regularly pays money to influential union leaders not to provoke the workers to call a strike or create havoc especially in the middle of important orders. The absence of labour organizations often led to chaos in the factory. For example, in one incident, three days before the Eid holiday some workers requested an advance on the next month's salary as they wanted to go home for extended leave. The production managers did not approve their request professionally and the workers were about to go on a strike. The owners went to the factory and checked the details of the workers who were eligible to get an extended leave with some financial benefits. The decision resolved the possibility of having a strike in the factory.

The owners usually do not visit the factory without a major issue which gives space to the mid-level management to violate the basic labour regulations such as the use of child labour. It seems that when there is a deadline to meet, momentous pressure is brought upon the workers by the managers. During a particularly large order with limited time, Das, one of the owners, visited the factory after midnight. He found that young children were working at midnight. He immediately called the manager on duty and asked him to clear out space in one of the empty rooms and prepare makeshift beds so that the children could sleep. The company itself did not employ any child labour, as the management argued, but in times of meeting deadline, hired children on contract for only that time to help speed up the process. The production manager allowed this because the job was not physically challenging – helping in folding the clothes, picking away stray threads from the spools, and stitching buttons. This happened without the owners' knowledge.

Overall the company is not happy with the workers and intends to shift to automation if affordable. Das shares that most factories face these common problems that need to be dealt with. There are unavoidable hassles created by the workers, but there are some which can be handled with more automation. Human error, intentionally or not intentionally, could be avoided with a move towards more reliance on advanced technology. The management is fed up with workers failing to follow the rules and needing to deal with the same issues all the time. According to the owner, "Workers have become more reckless in their behaviour and show no loyalty or honesty."

The factory is not affiliated with Accord, Alliance, and National Initiative. Without any certification of any agencies, the buying houses take advantage of the company. Texphin is more open to the exploitation of buying houses that continuously offer lower rates for the orders. The buying houses tend to oversee and interfere in the entire production process starting with fixing deals with others to get the fabric, dyes, and other materials even sometimes with higher prices than Texphin's sources. Choosing the right buyer is key to the survival of these smaller factories, knowing which agent will bring in the most returns with the least demands. Eventually, there are very little or no profits from buying house contracts. The factory management prefers subcontracts because they are profitable, and they can be more flexible with their work in order to get a better deal when it comes to the cost of production. However, it would be better if the factory gets direct orders from buyers, but still, they do not have this capacity. The orders for buying houses are mostly from buyers who do not mind the compliance status of the company. Meanwhile, the companies lean towards subcontracts from Malaysia and Saudi Arabia, who have a much better rate than others. Das

Table 4.2 Labour standard of small factories

Labour standard	*All factories (%)*	*Small factories (%)*
No CSR policy	29.05	19.08
Engage in subcontracting	16.56	11
Less labour productivity	26.71	16
No compliance audit	11.92	10.53
No CAPs	11.49	9.21
No WPC	23.18	19.08

Source: Management survey (2017–2018).

explains that the compliance factories have to invest about Tk. 5 crore in meeting the demands, but there is no assurance that this investment will turn into profit. The main obstacle is the tendency of buyers to squeeze the suppliers by offering continuously low prices. It requires a huge investment to fight the difficult challenges of the global market. The owner predicted that small factories could be shut down soon due to a lack of capacity. The biggest issue that remains, according to Das, is the corrupt governance of the state. The government needs to keep an eye on the small factories and help them flourish and sustain themselves by bringing in the latest machinery at a subsidized price and setting a standard for workers' training.

To sum up, the labour standard of Texphin supports the overall working conditions of the small factories explored in one of my research projects, conducted in 2016–2018 (see Table 4.2).[6] In this management survey, out of 152 factories, 35.33% were small, 41.33% medium, and 23.33% large.[7] The survey found that small factories were characterized by the absence of compliance audit, WPC, Corporate Social Responsibility (CSR) policy, and a safety action plan. Aligned with these findings, the case study shows Texphin did not comply with Accord, Alliance, or NI standards, thus its workplace safety was in question. The absence of approval is one of the key factors of not doing business with leading buyers with the capacity of offering large orders. For this reason, this factory worked with small orders with unstable buyers. As a result, the workers did not get the opportunity to work overtime and increase their earnings. The earning of workers was the low and the less earning was also the reason for the lowest job security, the highest labour turnover, and absenteeism in this company. But this is not the only reason for such unhealthy management–worker relations. Texphin did not have any kind of workers and management training facilities and the owners didn't think of training workshops as innovative and helpful in increasing skills. The differences of opinions between the senior management divided the workers as well, who preferred talking to one manager over another, bestowing varied levels of trust. Such a situation creates a disruption, even in the production line, since, when workers saw that the senior managers were undecided, they tended to exploit the situation to their own benefit. This happened especially because the company didn't allow its workers to form any kind of union and WPC. The tension between workers and mid-level management was so high that the workers tweaked the machinery so that production was delayed or quality decreased with the company failing to address such issues. Texphin was affected negatively in terms of job security, workers' payment, management–worker relations due to the lack of compliance and investment which were connected with having business with unstable buyers and subcontractors.

The first case study – Bantai – argues that it is very difficult for small factories to survive, even after offering good practices at the workplace. Welfare programmes of Bantai offered day-care service as well as education for the workers' children. A sizeable group of workers started working at Bantai due to the day-care service. Hajera Begum, for example, said that one of her main reasons for joining Bantai was the day-care service. She felt worried about leaving her baby at home. Later, she could work without any fear due to Bantai's day care. Another garment worker, Afreen, had two brothers and one sister who were educated in the Bantai School. As this school only covered primary education, Bantai agreed to arrange further education for them if they were interested. As a result of the Bantai closure, workers like Hajera and Afreen not only lost their jobs but also displaced the aspirations of family members of the next generation. In similar ways, other Bantai employees have been made vulnerable by the company's closure. These stories show that providing good practices in the workplace is one way of being competitive, but as is evidenced by the case study, this is not the only path to ensure sustained growth. One of the barriers to Bangladesh's small garment factories is limited knowledge in the marketing sector. The industry has developed through its network of subcontractors. A very limited number of small manufacturers maintain a direct channel to the buyers; the rest of the orders come through subcontracting, which takes away a good deal of profit. Institutions have not been established to provide training in the marketing sector. Without any marketing knowledge, the Bangladeshi small garment manufacturers will continue to be dependent on subcontractors. Bantai depended on its foreign partner to receive orders from the buyers. Bantai could have developed its marketing knowledge at that time to prepare itself but such preparation did not take place.

One of the challenges of the development of small factories like Texphin and Bantai is accessibility. The access of external stakeholders to these factories is limited. There are two reasons behind it: (1) small factories do not have any strategic relations with the big ones and (2) even if the door of opportunity opens in front of them, they can't usually grab it. They don't have mid-level management that will help the factories understand, internalize, and implement the strategic advice provided by an external agency. For instance, the BGMEA has come up with a funded project named "TREES" (Towards Resource Efficient and Environmental Sustainability) for small factories. From this experience, the BGMEA found that it is very difficult to work with small factories due to a lack of their proper resources, specialized engineers, and real desire to make changes. A BGMEA staff has shared his experience of working with a small factory:

> There was a factory with which I had to work with. PaCT gave them a list of light bulbs they need in their factory to save energy. Instead of listening to PaCT, they went with their ideology by buying an excess amount of tube lights just to make the factory look posh. Then, it was very difficult to make them understand that delicacy, brightness, and posh should not be the prime goal here. First, they need to produce goods in the factory at the lowest cost possible by reducing energy to earn the maximum amount of profit. This type of mentality is required to be changed.[8]

Also, small factories suffer from a shortage of money and a lack of knowledge of management practices. A culture of professionalism and buraucratic managemnt is missing in small factories. In most cases, it is a one-man show where a manager or owner controls everything regardless of the presence or absence of that skill. Some factory owners think that they've been running their business for a long time, so they can continue the same management style for the rest of their lives. A lot of them, having little or no knowledge about sustainability, usually tend to avoid the hassle of managing documents or paper works that are required to form policy. The mid-level management does not agree to run the line with modern thinking. They are not interested to change their traditional management system. They always like to say, "I am working in my way for the whole of life, I know the best." Such a mentality does not help for a change.

Notes

1 Focus group discussion with the researcher in December 2003.
2 Interview with the researcher, January 14, 2004.
3 Ranu, Bantai worker, focus group discussion with the researcher, December 2003–January 2004.
4 Interview with the researcher, January 14, 2004.
5 The case study of Texphin was conducted in 2018 as a part of a global research project by BIGD, BRAC University. Details are mentioned in end note 5.
6 The management survey was conducted in 2017–2018 as part of a research project. BRAC Institute of Governance and Development (BIGD) at BRAC University in collaboration with the London School of Economics, the University of New South Wales, the Freie University, the University of Gothenburg initiated a research titled, "Changes in the Governance of Garment Global Production Networks: Lead Firm, Supplier and Institutional Responses to the Rana Plaza Disaster." This three-year research project was funded by the Volkswagen Foundation with Wellcome Trust and Riksbanken Jubileumsfond as part of the Europe and Global Challenges Program. The author of this book was one of the

team members of the management survey. In the survey, senior factory management of 152 factories were interviewed.

7 Factories were categorized on the basis of size of workers. Small: 0–599, medium: 600–2,499, large: 2,500+.

8 See Chapter 7 for PaCT.

5 Case study

Medium and large factory

From the theoretical perspective, since the 1980s, there has been a trend away from traditional work practices to innovative work practices in many countries. Scholars have used a variety of terms to define "innovative work" – such as "high performance," "best practice" and "flexible work practices" (Ichnioswki et al., 1996; Kochan and Osterman, 1994). Kochan and Osterman (1994) have argued that if we invest more in human resources and improve organizational practices, the outcome will be higher productivity. One of the traditional strategies of firms to increase their competitiveness is to lower the price of their products by holding down wages. Through this strategy, they can gain productivity, but the living standard of most of the workforce is lowered. In contrast, the goal of a mutual gains enterprise is to follow the "high-road" strategy that is high productivity and high wages defined more generally by the authors as competitiveness at a high standard of living. Kochan and Osterman (1994) utilize the term "mutual gains" to describe best practices or "high road." The main goal of mutual gain is to ensure that any production gains are shared with employees. This sharing may be facilitated by offering more beneficial services to the workers. For example, decent wages, health and safety incentives, awards for performance, day care for employees' children, etc. can help workers to fully concentrate in the workplace. As a result, there will be fewer errors and employee turnover. According to Kochan and Osterman (1994), by following "mutual gains" the volume of production will not only increase, but there is also an effect on quality, innovation, timely delivery, and efficiency. The gains of improved productivity would then be distributed among the stakeholders. The job of stakeholders is to reinvest in human resources and therefore ensure improved standards of living for future generations

The view of Kochan and Osterman has been supported by other scholars such as Ichnioswki et al. (1996). Despite their views, the attitudes of management towards its workers may be regarded as paternalistic. In this regard, the organizational literature on modern methods of worker control criticizes the above-mentioned strategy. Scholars of modern methods of social control argue that employers implement indirect rather than coercive strategies of control in the workplace (Edwards, 1979; Hodson, 1999; Lincoln and

Kalleberg, 1990). This means that the social control of workers has moved away from direct control towards a more corporatist form whereby organizational structures are introduced to emphasize employees' commitment to an organization and to cultivate a sense of community in the workplace (Mueller, Coster and Ester, 2001). The process creates a misconception among the workers that they are free from control. In reality, management indirectly controls employees through this modern method of social control. As a result, satisfied workers are expected to, in turn, be more committed, cooperative, and motivated to work, which will lead to higher production and lower turnover in the organization (Mueller, Coster and Ester, 2001).

This theoretical approach is used in the case study of a medium factory "IMPTX" and a large factory known as "FRA." IMPTX started its journey in 2008 with its partners in Mirzapur, whereas FRA was established in 1998 in Narayangonj as a sole company. The total number of workers in IMPTX was 4,500, and the worker's size of FRA was 10,000. The annual turnover of FRA was twice that of IMPTX; $58 million for the latter and $120 million for the former. Despite these differences in capacity, both garment companies have maintained global core labour standards and because of this achievement, they do business with leading buyers such as H&M and have a long-term relationship with their buyers.

Compared to IMPTX, FRA has expanded its business within a short period. The turnover of FRA was three crore in 2001 and increased to eight crores within two years due to the construction of a ten-storeyed building production unit. Again, in 2005, the annual turnover jumped to 12 crores because of expanding a four-storeyed production building to six-storeyed. By 2007 the earning was around 16 crores, and in 2008 there was another ten-storeyed building unit which was 14–15 thousand square feet, so the turnover was 30 crore by then, almost double, and up until 2014 it gradually increased to about 65 crores. In 2015, there was another leap to about 91 crores, with a 37% growth, as all the floors were finally equipped and production was maximized, Later FRA started the business with a new buyer, UK's biggest brands, Primark. As a result of more orders from existing and new buyers and expansion of factory units the turnover was 120 million dollars in 2017. The Executive Director (ED) of the company describes the company as a "maverick" kind. This is because the company did not have a specific goal in mind, as to when and by how much they will increase or achieve. The opportunities came up and the company decided whether or not to invest. According to the ED, "I want the transformation in FRA to be reflected in the countrywide industry. I want the industry to flourish in and of itself, through the factories staying interconnected and in positive or productive competition with each other." How the FRA and IMPTX were operated is explained in the following sections (Table 5.1).

Table 5.1 Labour relations of IMPTX and FRA

IMPTX	*FRA*
Workers size 4,500, annual turnover U.S.$58 million Lead buyers: H&M, Marks& Spencer, Zara Certified by Accord, BSCI, eight audits per year Formal contracts with workers The average tenure of workers three years Average wage Tk. 6,000 Absenteeism 5% labour turnover 5% WPC present but, no safety committee or union	Established 1998 Knit composite, Workers size 10,000, Annual turnover $120 million Lead Buyers: H&M 37%, C&A 23%, Primark 12% Certified by Accord, WRAP, BSCI, OEKO-TEX, GOTS, OCS, GRS. 15–20 audits in a year Formal contract with piece rate and salary workers Average tenure six years Average wage Tk. 6,272 Absenteeism 5% labour turnover 2.43% WPC and safety committee present. No union

Source: Management survey (2017–2018).

5.1 Management–worker relationship

The companies pay workers' wages, bonuses, and overtime within the first seven days of the month. All of them are permanent workers; there are no contract-based workers in the factories. The two companies are now in the process of paying salaries through a digital payment method. There is no union but has the Workers Participation Committee (WPC). Justifying the absence of union the management argued that, some union leaders provoke the workers to rebel against the factories. But labour law is maintained in this both garment company and all payments are following the government rules. Especially since there are safety committees and WPCs the influence of outsiders has been compromised. The management organized an election to form the WPC committee in the presence of buyer and government authority and provided all the necessary resources such as room, the ballot box, and even continuous video recording of the election. The buyers were present on the day of the election and the election fantastically took place. The WPC holds a meeting every month and the senior management listens to the problems of the workers to avoid protest of workers. One sign of workers' protest is evident in FRA i.e. the issue of different attendance bonuses by different levels of workers. The issue was shared by the WPC with the top management in a meeting. Now they are hopeful that it will be resolved. However, the workers seemed used to the use of verbal abuse. The workers believe that the level of verbal abuse is not serious but there should be some sort of verbal abuse in the factory to fulfil the target; it is natural and very much not at the level of oppressive. Though these factories are large firms in Bangladesh, very few incidents are there related to their workers' issues. They have maintained workers' laws and payment schedules; thus, external pressure from different people could not harm the company that much. The active cooperation of the safety committee and WPC has made this possible.

There are complaint boxes in the factory, and the common issues reported are: the shower is not working in the bathroom; male co-workers are smoking in the bathroom; and sometimes the bathroom has become smelly, the water of "Ozu" (ablution) entering through the floor. The management also receives complaint such as male workers disturb the female for having affair. Hence, solving those problems might get difficult for management. In FRA, there was a complaint filed by a female doctor on account of sexual harassment, and the letter she used was sent directly to the Accord office. Eventually, this was proven to be false allegations after an investigation was carried out by Accord. Several workers keep placing complaints and many times it is false, so keeping a track of this, or investigating these issues over and over is quite impossible, as stated by the factory management. In this context, the line supervisor of FRA says, "There aren't many problems in our company. The workplace is relatively safe. However, if there is any issue then there is the HR department, which takes immediate investigations and actions as per the law."

All the issues of workers are recorded including maternity leave and payment in a document file because these are also overseen by the buyers to ensure that there are no false allegations. Dealing with workers has changed a lot since the beginning when work could be completed through different workers on different days, and there were fewer rules. But more recently, with the labour law and all, the steps are quite elaborate, with 1st, 2nd, and so on notices being sent before any action can be taken up against any of the workers. Besides, they have to be given the proper severance fees and benefits and these are cross-checked via their files.

The labour turnover is low in these two companies. This is because they have an assurance that getting the order is not a problem for the companies, and the continuity of order ensures the availability of job for workers. In FRA there are 5 floors dedicated to sewing and a total of 120 sewing lines, and 117 production lines. The total number of workers is about 10,000. All the workers bring their food from their homes but they do have a canteen. So during their breaks, they can relax either near their machines, in the canteen, or even outside the factory. Both male and female workers are treated and managed in the same way and sometimes offer incentives or motivations. For example, there is a project from the World Bank where they give mothers Tk. 1,000 per month to buy milk, so they forward this month through the factory, and it is then sent to their bank accounts at Pubali Bank, these accounts were opened for the workers by FRA using just Tk. 10 per head. So they receive money directly. The IMPTX gives incentives to the workers based on a certain level of production such as completing

50–60% of the production, and so most of the workers avail themselves the incentive since workers are always doing more than 50%. The workers are also motivated to get an efficiency incentive. Anyone doing more than 50% efficiency gets cash. Also, the workers get breakfast - bread, banana, and egg - when they enter the factory. Because of these incentives, the skill of the workers is better than before. Both companies have a training centre where any helper who joins as a new member is trained to be proficient and skilful as well as professionally dressed. The helpers then are trained up to become an operator. The management takes an operator from outside as well as create operators in the factory through training. Countries like Cambodia is much more efficient compared to Bangladesh. Even though workers are lacking behind in terms of education, the workers' skills have improved a lot compared to previous times.

Although the companies provide different resources for workers, they are not satisfied with the efficiency of their workers.[1] In the present status of the $500 billion global industry, China holds about $200 billion; Bangladesh holds about $28 billion; and Vietnam holds $25 billion and is predicted to soon supersede the market share of Bangladesh. This is because, as management says, the industry has some infrastructural problems and a deficiency of skilled workforce.

Box 5.1 A supervisor's tale

Rubel has been working at FRA for about four years. He started as a worker in the quality checking department, but, since he had to work night shifts, he wanted to leave the job. The company appointed him as an input supervisor. Currently, he is earning Tk. 18,000 per month. Explaining how the production is processed, Rubel mentions that when the sample is given, the supervisors receive some slips that need to be submitted to the sub store available on each floor. From here, the supervisor collects all the accessories, such as labels, that are required for the finished product, and then these are distributed amongst the workers. The fabric needs to be folded and then taken to the next worker, and this work is done by the production operator. Then, the supervisor must look at the garment and check the procedure that has to be completed, for example, the shoulder cut requires an overclock to be done, so these have to be ascertained and instructed to the workers.

The production lines are mostly organized according to the product sample, with one floor sometimes having 12 lines and other times having 4. In these lines, machines are also arranged according to the sample, with over 25 sewing machines being set up at a time. So, once the operators are set up, there is hourly production monitoring. This is not done for the finished product itself, in that this happens after every step of the operation, with everybody sewing at once and the count being says 150/180 pieces for a certain task within that hour, such as shoulder setting or collar cutting, etc. These tasks have to be thoroughly monitored with these hourly targets being written down in the notebooks or proper files.

Rubel also shares instances in which the workers themselves become advisers to the owners or the top management and share innovative ideas based on their own experiences. As an example, for leggings, they had improvised the process that had saved a lot of time. So, time spent on leggings is reduced, while there is an increase in production. There are other examples too, such as with the label, which used to be separately sewed and is now put underneath the fold and fixed onto the clothes using just one top-sewing procedure; more worker contact in the processes means better quality since the products are made based on human judgements. These changes have enhanced the quality of the products.

When an operator slows down or does not meet their target, he/she needs to be monitored and advised with care, without scolding or condescending so that they are not offended. Rubel explains that sometimes he shows how the steps are to be done quickly or efficiently, and when that does not work out he brings another operator from a different line or position and places them next to the worker who has lost motivation. This prompts a feeling of competition since they are paid on piece rate; since the other worker is taking away all their production capability and pieces, the workers speed up production, and the targets are met on an hourly basis. To overcome the boredom and monotony, proper breaks are given, at 11 a.m. and then at lunch, and there is a huge canteen where workers can go.

Source: Management survey (2017–2018).

5.2 Buyer–supplier relationships

Usually, buyers first come and check the available facilities of factories, such as dyeing, labs, machinery, and buildings. They emphasize the establishment of labs, which help ensure quality. Having a lab conveys a positive impression about a supplier because it means that the factory can ensure the quality of the production. Moreover, the compliance score is checked by the buyers as well. Initially, the buyers of IMPTX and FRA were very ordinary. The leading buyers such as H&M, C&A, Target Australia, Zara, and Primark have started doing business with these two companies after convincing of the size of the factory buildings, working capacity, and compliance. Alam, the owner of IMPTX, said, there are allegations that garment owners use expensive cars but one of the uses of these cars is for the buyers when they come to Bangladesh. Receiving the buyers from the airport to dropping them off at the hotel and again taking them to factory visit, for all these kinds of purposes, expensive cars are used. In some cases, a helicopter takes the buyers to factories and other places so that they do not have to face the traffic jam. The buyers are happy with the hospitality offered by the suppliers in Bangladesh. According to Alam, even after all the political unrest and problems in Bangladesh, the buyers are continuing their relationship with his company because of the hospitality apart from quality products.

As a result of this good relationship, when the company is in a problem regarding the delivery of the product in due time, the buyer extends cooperation. Long-time buyers and suppliers are mutually dependent on one another on good and bad days; as the owner of the IMPTX said:

> Suppose H&M ordered something, but then they might say that they do not want the particular order but instead they want something different. In a situation like this where I have already bought the thread and I might face loss because of this decision. However, I still go with the buyer's request and will hold the product and from next consignment, I will adjust the cost with the buyer.

However, the relationship that the company has with H&M is not the same as that with other buyers. H&M gives LC to the company for the whole year, whereas other buyers do not provide those facilities, no matter how big they are, which is a problem of doing business. With very few buyers, the management has a healthy business relationship. Because the volume of the order is always large in number, often not less than 1 million pieces and hardly any need for change in style. It is easier for the workers to produce the same product in large quantities rather than producing different products in smaller quantities. Working with this type of buyer, labour productivity is always higher. With other buyers, the management has to face the problem of frequent change of factory layout because of the variety of the product which at the end of the day affects labour efficiency.

The factory management also shares its vulnerability to buyers, particularly decreasing prices from buyers. According to IMPTX, the price that the buyers offer has come down by 50% compared to what it was five years back. Still, the factory is running because the volume of the order has increased. Suppose, the company, five years back received 10,000 pieces of order from H&M but now has increased to 1 million. Because of this increase in the volume the company is still able to do business. Five years back the factory would produce a basic t-shirt for 2.5 dollars, whereas now, it does the same for one dollar 20 cents or even 1 dollar. Alam, the owner of IMPTX, says that the owners and the buyers have learned many things in the past which are allowing them to be cost-efficient and still having profit where the price has decreased. FRA also goes through the same experience.

After the Rana Plaza, the cost of compliance has increased significantly mainly due to Accord and Alliance. For a large company like FRA, it needs to earn at least 4 million pieces of garments work order per month to meet up the operation cost. The profit margin is also decreasing since there is very little bargaining that can be done with the buyers. Retaining a 5% profit margin now is difficult, while in 2002, there was 15% of profit margin as the company owner stated. Sometimes it turns out that with particular buyers they have to incur a negative profit return at times. Yet, production must go on, as leaving the big company's capacity unutilized is more harmful than the loss incurred, so the cost of production has increased as well. The Managing Director (MD) of FRA describes the vulnerability of supplier in dealing with a leading buyer:

> Whereas in the past 2 years they [buyer] had taken about 2 tons of work for $2 per piece, and now they ask for a lower price. The buyer announced at a meeting of suppliers that they have about 30 million orders to place and that whoever can take as much might do so. However, once a factory says that they can work a certain amount, they are asked about the rate of payment, for example, FRA had to go down from $2 to $1.80. This happens as there is no or little unity amongst owners, who continuously want more work for their selves, so they reduce prices to make their offer more lucrative so that buyers would give them the work. So there is uncertainty around this as well, as, if someone offers less price rate they tend to get the bulk orders, which are required for the business to keep running. Then there is another issue with offering a lower price rate, in that buyers will then give them most or more work than they wanted, like about 10 million of work instead of the required 5–6 million pieces of work, and this would result in a loss as well, but the owners cannot refuse as this would hamper reputation, and in extreme cases, buyers might be so frustrated that they refuse to place any order at all.

Smaller factories' owners tend to blame the bigger factories' owners for their recurring failure to accommodate orders and also price rates as the bigger factories agree to lower prices but for smaller ones, working at this rate is very harmful. This could have been avoided if simply there were some solidarity amongst the owners. Thus, all of the blame cannot be put on the buyers, where the owners of factories are so ready to reduce prices to ensure that they acquire the business.

The strategy of these two companies regarding the buyer's relation is straightforward. The factories are driven by the buyers' demands the buyers set the tone in the market. What the factory owners must do is get the answers ready for all the concerns of buyers – the uncertainties in the safety issues, worker relations, and even political instability. A high level of assurance is driven by the positive relations built up over the years through constant trade and established goodwill. This relationship is so inclusive that the buyers also feel they can patronize the production and service strategies employed by even such an established and reputable company, and this is appreciated, in turn, since it allows the company to understand the needs of the buyers and thus become more specialized in providing services for them. The market is thus run by buyers, and the Bangladeshi RMG sector is dependent on them. The market will only then be run by suppliers when the competence level of suppliers is that high or efficient, for example, the way China is running, and the way Vietnam is approaching.[2]

5.3 Management strategy

The RMG sector of Bangladesh is essentially both at secondary and tertiary levels of production, as they buy certain products from elsewhere, assemble those in Bangladesh, and then sell that finished goods to buyers. To improve the level of competence thus, there is a need for some flagships. For instance, diversifying the production is likely to result in profits. With Zara as a buyer for FRA, they are hoping that they can shift production towards other products, such as fleeces, jackets, prints, or even embroidery. The adhering to basic products, where there is a lot of competition, has become null in bringing in profits. However, compared to diversify the product, the difficult job is management control. In FRA there are board meetings every two months where everyone from the top management level can engage in an open discussion about the advantages and disadvantages they are facing through the employment or application of various strategies; there are also yearly meetings with all levels of managerial posts. The MD of the company usually sits with the senior general managers and the management meetings with several departments' staffs are held by the ED, a key person in running the factory.

Inspired by Vivek Anand, the ED believes, "We only seem busy and our lives are shrouded in that illusion, while in reality, this is nothing more than the consequences of being disorganized." He explains that the entire RMG industry in Bangladesh is suffering from this disorganized status and so there is this constant pull of work, with issues popping up at any point in time and which need to be dealt with immediately. This is a direct effect of the Bangladeshi culture, as the ED claims, and this sense of business needs to be pipe-lined into a productive kind. For example, the lunch break is always time-consuming because workers and staff take more than scheduled time excusing for attending prayer before or after lunch. The superiors or subordinates in the workplace deal with this problem when there are a set of rules and regulations that can be referred to for all kinds of workplace issues. A culture of professionalism needs to be placed – both IMPTX and FRA are working on it.

A unique management approach of FRA is the introduction of a Management Training Unit (MTU) that trains about 150 young university graduates from leading universities of Bangladesh to bring a transformation in technological mind-set in the factory. Explaining the necessity of this unit, the ED says,

> This is my time to give back to the industry, to do something for the betterment and persistence of the industry, because there is a lot of untapped talent, which can help in flourishing the companies and the industry at large.

In other words, it is necessary to bring about a shift in the approach of factory management – the generation and process of the new idea using digital technology. According to the company, the younger generation thinks and works differently from the current general managers who are from the older generation. This youth group excels in their work and overcomes the repetitions and redundancies of the older style of working out problems and resolving issues. The young trainees do bring in a lot of ideas and assistance for the company. For example, FRA now maintains TA (Time and Action plan), a platform with several databases within it such as the Enterprise Resource Planning (ERP), which cannot be controlled by the older members of the company, as the senior management argued. Meanwhile, a young energetic staff hands in an analytical dashboard daily, and it is so concise that just by glancing at a single page, everyone could understand whether or not the factory and all the departments within it are running smoothly. Since data is the emerging game-changer in the market, the company considers the youth as the main resource to bring in and execute a modern management approach. However, retaining these fresh talents is quite difficult for the company because of their nature to shift to another job or a better lifestyle. The older staffs are also jealous of this emerging youth in the company. Keeping a fixed strategy is less helpful for the FRA in such cases than implementing various tactics, especially thinking about the long-term sustainability of any effective strategy. The company invites the young generation to select their jobs according to how what, and where they can contribute so that, in turn, the job can itself fulfil their individual needs automatically.

Both companies – IMPTX and FRA – believe in a philosophy that they need to have people who are happy in the workplace as one of the senior management states: "I suggest smiling during work, to remember that this place is a happy place and to send that message across to others as well." But making everyone happy is a great challenge for senior management. One of the weaknesses of both companies is mid-level management. Although key actors of the companies including lead buyers come forward to offer training for workers and managers there is a gap in the training of mid-level management, particularly in HR and compliance. In FRA there are three levels of authority – Board members, EDs to GMs and managers, and assistant managers. For the conversation to be initiated, all three levels of authority have to be present at the same hour to discuss the issues from the root level. Despite this mechanism, there has been a lot of office politics going on among the staff of different departments. One major issue is that there is mistrust between the top-level management and the mid-level management. To resolve this, the FRA is trying to evoke a level of dignity amongst the staff as well as workers. To do this, one needs to trust each other, share information, and delegate work. In this way, the top management believes that establishing a transparent mechanism in the company may overcome the distrust with each other. To the company, decentralized power is also essential, where hoarding information is no longer the case and so there would be no office politics and grudges held against each other owing to a hierarchical system. A system of transparency needs to be established and micromanaging needs to be overcome, only then, as the company believes, can there be trust in the workplace.

The workers and even supervisors also receive some training. To inspire workers, the management has introduced a strategy called "motivational speaking."' There is a 5-minute assembly each morning in FRA where each supervisor gives a speech to 20–25 workers telling them not to be absent and to maintain workplace etiquette and other rules such as wearing masks, using scissors and cutters, not using earphone during work as this causes distraction and increases the rate of mistakes. Also in these meetings, the supervisors discuss the output targets, compare daily output, and emphasize labour productivity. The supervisors are trained by the production managers to motivate workers. One of these tactics involves disseminating good news to everyone. For example, if there is a sudden bonus for meeting the target, this message needs to be passed along. The training centre also teaches workers how to use the compliance scissor cutter, what the quality policies are, and other issues of the workplaces.

Another management strategy is competition amongst the supervisors. During the training of supervisors, they are taught to reduce time in the movement of materials, maintain their aisle mark, and be careful while handling sharp tools, explain the entire process so that there are no mistakes or rejects as these incur losses. Commissions are given to the supervisors based on how many rejection rates and whether there were any complaints from the workers against the supervisor. Even as the companies shift towards automation, workers are trained to operate the machines.

To adapt to different challenges, innovation is also taking place. IMPTX has set up an office in Italy where the owner has appointed designers so that they are aware of the latest designs of clothing and get familiar with the upcoming design style. Whatever is trending to buyers, the factory starts producing them by the virtue of the advancement of technology. Previously the cutting was done by hand but now it is fully done by machine. Thus, the waste is much less compared to hand cutting, and as a result, the cost has been reduced. Since the GSP will be withdrawn in 2025, the FRA is thinking about new ways to make the industry more stable and competitive in the global market.[3] To make the company, the management strategies include moving towards newer technology, more automation, a technological transformation in the structure and organization of businesses, having on board a designing team consisting of 10–12 Chinese designers and one Indian designer, and new product innovation.

Both IMPTX and FRA support the appointment of foreign staff in the industry to fill up the deficiency of highly skilled professionals in this sector as well as a cultural factor. To the senior management of both companies, there is a huge difference between foreigners and Bangladeshi employees in respect of skills. Their mentalities are better than the Bangladeshi mid-level management – open to new things and highly professional. The interpersonal relationship plays a huge role for the local staff which is less important to foreigners. According to senior management, for example,

> Before the GM (General Manager) was ordained, a Bangladeshi was in that post as a DGM (Deputy General Manager). Previously he worked in another sector but he worked hard and as a reward, he was moved to a more important unit. But unfortunately, after getting the promotion he became very ruthless, exercising power unnecessarily and his attitude became so presumptuous that he did not allow his subservient staff to enter his cabin with shoes on and was reluctant to share his allotted car with other staffs during official traveling. These are some basic examples of the mentality of the Bengali people. Perhaps his case was an extreme one. The local employees are not generous enough to teach their fellow workers the skills that he/she is adroit at, fearing it would make their positions vulnerable. But they never ponder on the fact that there is a position beyond their positions. Knowledge is an incremental thing. No one can mug it from another. The foreign staffs are very expensive but amicable in this regard and open to new things.

Another reason for attracting foreign staff is the inadequate local supply of highly skilled professionals. The Bangladesh RMG industry started its journey in 1978, and 41 years later, we are still heavily dependent on imported skills at the management level. It seems foreigners are keener to get into our garments sector than us. Around 13% of the country's garments factories have employed foreign experts in the top posts who remit over $5 billion from Bangladesh every year (CPD, 2018). In the absence of a skilled workforce, particularly in merchandising, design, and marketing, as well as in the operation of sophisticated machines, the factory owners have hired experts from China, Taiwan, Japan, Sri Lanka, and India to fill the gap. There is no harm in embracing the knowledge of foreign workers. But it is also a matter of frustration that we have failed to supply the domestic resources to occupy these positions.

5.4 Government support

The garment entrepreneurs, like the owners of IMPTX and FRA, strongly believe that without this sector, Bangladesh cannot survive because of the reliance of more than 4 million workers, directly or indirectly; financial organizations; insurance companies; transport; and, above all, women workers. To sustain the growth of the export-oriented garment industry, a crucial role needs to be played by the government. According to Alam,

> When a woman worker is entering a garment factory, she is getting 10,000 taka and with that taka, she is supporting a family. If this industry fall all these female workers will come to the street. They do not have any other way of earning. So in order to compete with the world, the garment owners need to build the factory in that way and they need government help for that.

But the demands of workers that they be protected from unsafe working conditions via reforming legislation and strengthening capacity building had rarely been addressed by the government until the building collapse in Rana Plaza. A study by Rahman (2019) summarizes some key achievements of the government. The amendments to the Bangladesh Labor Act (BLA) 2006 include training and provisions of safety equipment, mandatory fire drills, reports of accidents to authority, finance to treat sick employees, compensation for worker death, labour inspection programmes, elected participation committee, and the National Occupational Safety and Health Policy 2013. For the capacity building of the government, the National Tripartite Plan of Action was prepared to oversee factory building safety, the Department of Inspection for Factories and Establishments (DIFE) inspected 1549 factories and Remediation Coordination Cell was formed. The number of inspectors has been increased from 183 pre-Rana Plaza to 575 post-Rana Plaza, and the budget was increased from \$0.97 million before 2013 to \$4.1 million in 2015–2016 (Shipar, 2017).

Among different government initiatives, the senior management of IMPTX and FRA was particularly concerned with Section 205 of the BLA 2006, which requires employers hiring more than 50 workers in any establishments to set up an elected "participation committee" (PC). The management survey (2017–2018) finds that 78% of senior management reported the presence of a PC in their factory and 70% of these PCs included elected workers' representatives. Although the PC has engaged workers of each factory to discuss their issues directly with the management without any interference from the outsiders, the presence of PC has challenged trade unions since very few factories have unions (Rahman, 2019). However, all garment owners who participated in the management survey including the owners of IMPTX and FRA were satisfied with the management-PC relationship. To the management, it seems the overwhelming presence of PC in the factory has overshadowed the justification of having a union in the workplace. According to the management of FRA, "...there are few union leaders who tried to provoke the workers to labour unrest although the factory strictly follows labour laws. After the formation of PC, such political influence from outsiders is checked." While the management appreciated the government's initiative of elected PC, this kind of positive tone did not appear in the frustration generated by the factory inspection of the Accord and Alliance. The management expected the direct intervention of the government to make this transnational governance accountable to the sovereign state. According to the ED of FRA, "Raising a question about the way Accord was operated is essential, and in fact, Accord should be audited internationally to check why the costs of remediation was so expensive." Criticizing the government, the management claims that the government has channelled unlimited power to the Accord.

To be competitive in the global market, the factory management also emphasizes the role of the government in getting market access with favourable terms. Already the U.S. cancelled the GSP advantage for Bangladesh as a reaction to the Rana Plaza disaster. As an LDC, Bangladesh has received zero duty export to the EU under the EBA's (Everything but Arms) agreement. The EBA is treated as a GSP facility for the export of Bangladesh RMG to the EU countries and it is one of the key factors behind the rapid increase of export earnings from the EU since 2010. But this favourable term is going to be terminated in 2027 due to the graduation to a Lower-Middle-Income country. Still, with new status, Bangladesh can get the benefits of duty-free access under GSP-Plus if the country complies with the core UN conventions on labour reforms, human rights, and governance. The factory management argues that one way to convince the EU is to showcase the achievements the government so far earned from the "Sustainability Compact." Following the Rana Plaza incident in 2013, the EU took action through a "sustainability compact" jointly with Bangladesh, the ILO, and the U.S., aimed at improving labour, health, and safety conditions for workers as well as responsible behaviour by businesses within the industry (Rahman, 2019). The EU expected the government of Bangladesh to comply with 17 points. Although significant progress has been made by the government, the EU believes that more efforts need to be invested in the following issues: (a) regulations implementing the amendments of the Bangladesh Labour Act, (b) government delays in completing inspections and hiring additional inspectors, (c) slow response to unfair labour practices, and (d) labour reforms for EPZ (The Daily Star, 2017). This is a major concern of the factory management to ensure market access with favourable treatment.

From a very small earning at the beginning to a million-dollar company proves these companies' capacity into managing the business very efficiently. Both FRA and IMPTX have started their plan to expand the capacity which will boost their business and reputation along with their efficiency. The main success point of the companies is having a workforce that is managed professionally through various programmes of the management. The companies are also working towards future challenges. The job security and workers' pay are connected with better management–worker relations, concern for factory building safety, space for worker representation. The management–worker relationship is well in both case studies. For instance, the company pays its workers within the first seven days of the month who have formal job contracts, provides incentives as per performance, complimentary breakfast for punctual workers, routine audits, etc. As a result of such a working environment, the absenteeism and labour turnover is lower, the job security and average pay of workers are higher than average factories. Besides, the positive labour outcomes have been made possible due to the maintenance of compliance at the factory as well as WPC formation. The workers are satisfied with their wages because they also get, apart from a better workplace, sufficient overtime work to earn more. It means the buyers are giving more orders to the company under the satisfaction of audit regulation. However, IMPTX would be in a better position if the company had committed to more effective worker representation and voice by including a safety committee. Overall, the companies have successfully generated a more skilful taskforce but thrive to further this progress with additional training and labour organization which allows them to also step up on the ladder. Compared with IMPTX, FRA is better in different ways. It has the lowest labour turnover and absenteeism and highest job security, workers' pay, number of audits, the progress of remediation (98% completed) in building safety. All of these positive management strategies have attracted the leading buyers to expand their business with FRA. The company takes on expansion readily and cohesively, so that as the buyers' demands increase, they would be able to provide and meet the orders. They also plan and set particular goals which helps them to decide upon which investments to enter. Workers at FRA tend to stay back and so the labour turnover is not so high. This is because they have an assurance that there will be work in the company Similarly, the workers' opinions and strategies are taken into account through effective WPC and safety committee since they are thought of as the ones who are on the ground level and thus observe the daily operations and might be able to find a more efficient system. Incentives for workers, including overtime consideration and performance, are offered in both companies.

Following the theory of Kochan and Osterman (1994) the two case studies of this chapter establish that the success of any company depends on "high-road strategy" – good employer behaviour, concerning management in the workplace, training for workers, safe and secure working conditions, human resource development, ensuring workers' rights and other services for the workers. As articulated in this chapter, the economic and political context of the country is not favourable for the two garment companies to do business, especially when, mainly due to Accord and Alliance, the remediation cost has gone up but the price offered by the buyers is going down. Still, the growth is higher, even while accepting a lower profit margin. But the companies are optimistic about the future – order is coming to Bangladesh, and one needs to be competitive to grab the upcoming opportunity by focussing on product diversity, capacity building, innovative management practices, and strengthening human resources. The leading buyers are also dependable on these two companies and doing business for a decade. Both IMPTX and FRA take on expansion readily and cohesively so that as the buyers' demands increase, they would be able to provide and meet the orders. They also plan and set particular goals which helps them to decide upon which investments to enter. So the future is estimated and regarded accordingly. In this light, the companies are not afraid of diversifying either, and including newer designs, clothes, and machinery to decrease the risk of failure with changing global tastes and demands. In terms of responsibility towards the future, they take on training and seminars where the youth is especially addressed and consequently trained to deal with real-life issues at the workplace and encouraged to come up with innovative mannerisms to deal with the issues. With their dyeing and lab facilities, besides others, the buyers feel especially comfortable trusting towards the suppliers' operations. Also, an open discussion among the managers with the presence of top management is encouraged because this is the way to integrate different departments and avoid corporate politics. They also hold management meetings regularly where everyone in the top management can share their opinion about the plan of the company. The companies also pay close attention to the gaps between mid-level management and workers. It is very hard to control the mid-level management, and thus the company holds meeting regularly to sort out problems in communication.

Following the "high-road" strategy, the compliance department has become proactive to meet up the demands required to have a better score in the audit/code of conduct. The companies are very supportive of the buyers' code of conduct although the code of conduct varies from one buyer to another. During the case study, it was noticed that the compliance manager was following up on the decision taken in the last meeting with his staff and investigating whether the decisions of the last meeting were implemented or not. There are, of course, the HR departments attached to these companies, which are actively involved in maintaining a high-quality and safe work environment. The workers' opinions and strategies are taken into account since they are thought of as the ones who are on the ground level and thus observe the daily operations and might be able to find a more efficient system. The workers are initiated within the workplace through training and daily assemblies where they are given information about incentives. There is friendly competition amongst workers so that the work environment itself pushes workers to perform well and increase output. Routine check-ups within the hour allow no space for lacking in output and keeps workers in check. It is a shared responsibility to make sure everyone knows about any news or notices. The workers all receive proper breaks to enjoy their food and also rest, and the space within the premises allows for workers to rejuvenate themselves during the breaks. Since the labour laws are followed in these two companies, especially with a WPC in function, there are fewer complaints from the workers.

Notes

1 See Chapter 7 for reasons of lower labour productivity.
2 See Chapter 7 for further discussion of buyer – supplier relationship.
3 Since Bangladesh has graduated from LDC to Lower-Middle-Income country, it will not get trade advantages as an LDC from 2025 onwards.

6 Transnational governance

Accord and Alliance

The movements of national and global unions, along with other organizations working in labour rights, to prevent accidents in the Bangladesh export-oriented garments industry gained momentum after the Tazreen fire. In response, two approaches were offered: (a) "Memorandum of Understanding" for brands to invest in factory building safety in Bangladesh by the Worker Rights Consortium and the Clean Clothes Campaign, and (b) a Global Social Compliance Programme by the German Development Agency (Reinecke and Donaghey, 2015). Shortly after the collapse of Rana Plaza, an incident that sparked public outcry around the world, the unions, social movement organizations, and brands met in Germany to discuss both approaches. After a constructive discussion, the labour organizations ended up with the idea of a binding agreement to ensure the financial responsibility of buyers, and independent transparent inspections of factories (Reinecke and Donaghey, 2015). On behalf of unions, NGOs, and social movement organizations, the IndustriALL and UNi Global Union negotiated with the buyers to agree with their proposed approach. The situation was favourable for the global unions to convince the buyers and the government of Bangladesh. The Rana Plaza calamity led to enormous public pressure on Western retailers to come out with an immediate action plan to improve working conditions (Anner, 2015; Reinecke and Donaghey, 2015; Zajak, 2017). The government of Bangladesh was also under public and political pressure, along with realizing that the future of the leading export earning sector would be at stake. The situation was further intensified when the U.S. suspended the Generalised System Preferences (GSP) facility for Bangladesh (Bhadily, 2015). Under the heated environment and circumstances, the Bangladesh government extended its commitment of cooperation with the Accord on Fire and Building Safety in Bangladesh (Accord), and the Alliance for Bangladesh Worker Safety (Alliance).

6.1 Accord–Alliance framework

The Accord was an independent, legally binding agreement between brands and trade unions designated to work towards a safe and healthy Bangladeshi

Ready-Made Garments (RMG) Industry. It was a five-year agreement (2013–2018) that was extended after court proceedings until May 2020 (Bair et al., 2020). The Accord covered 1,670 factories and 218 European buyers were the members of the Accord. To be a member of the Accord, they paid a certain fee (starting from $500,000 and increasing each year), which was then used for inspection and remediation measures. These buyers were the driving force of the Accord, together with two global union federations (IndustriALL and UNIGlobal), and guidance by the ILO. The other signatories included local union – Bangladesh Textile and Garments Workers League, Bangladesh Revolutionary Garments Workers Federation, etc. Witness signatories for the project were Workers Right Consortium, International Labour Rights Forum, Clean Clothes Campaign, and Maquila Solidarity Network – all of whom are deeply involved in promoting labour and industry rights. The agreement became consolidated immediately after the Rana Plaza incident, and its six major components included:

i A five-year legally binding agreement (2013–2018) between trade unions and brands, to ensure a safe working environment in the Bangladesh's RMG industry.
ii Independent inspection programmes are supported by brands in which workers and trade unions are involved.
iii Public disclosure of Bangladesh's RMG factories, reports of inspections, and corrective action plans (CAPs).
iv A commitment by signatory brands to ensure that sufficient funds are available for remediation and maintaining sourcing relationships.
v Health and safety committees that are democratically elected in all factories, to identify and act on health and safety risks.
vi Worker empowerment through extensive training programmes, complaint mechanisms, and right to refuse work in unsafe environments.

On the other hand, the Alliance for Bangladesh Worker Safety ("Alliance") was a similar five-year commitment (2013–2018) to improve safety in the Bangladesh's RMG factories. The Alliance was established in 2013 through the Bipartisan Policy Center, U.S. chaired by former U.S. Senate majority leader George Mitchell and former senator Olympia Snowe. Similar to the Accord, the Alliance was also a collaborative process that involves companies and stakeholders including the U.S. and Bangladeshi governments, NGOs, policymakers, members of civil society as well as organized labour. In essence, the Alliance represented a majority of North American companies and institutions. The vision of Alliance was to improve worker safety in Bangladesh's RMG industry by educating workers and management, upgrading factories, empowering workers, and finally building institutions that can enforce and maintain safe working conditions throughout Bangladesh. The Alliance had 890 sole affiliate factories, until its closure in December 2018. The Alliance was supported by 29 buyers, all but one based in the U.S. Supporting associations included BRAC, Canadian Apparel Federation, United States Association of Importers of Textiles and Apparel, etc. Li Fung severs in an advisory capacity for the Alliance. Individual members had committed to a total of $100 million in accelerated access to low-cost capital to help factory owners in making factory safety improvements (Alliance, 2016).

The differences between these two initiatives have been analyzed by Donaghey and Reinecke (2018). The Accord, as argued by Donaghey and Reinecke (2018), reflects the democratic participation of worker representatives along with the obligation of corporations to constituent groups – a combination of Industrial Democracy and CSR. As from industry self-regulation, the Alliance is rooted in the principles of CSR. The inclusion of workers in the central body has made the Accord a pluralist approach while a unitarist approach is followed by the Alliance after the involvement of worker representatives in an advisory body. Both initiatives have opted for a credible enforcement mechanism to ensure compliance in the factory leaving behind flexible voluntary auditing. The legally binding nature of the Accord has created an environment of transparency and accountability in the process of inspection. The inclusion of strong action, such as termination for non-compliant factories, has made the new approaches of governance much more effective. According to the management survey, in case of factory closure, employers paid workers' compensation in Accord-affiliated factories, but buyers and employers shared the compensation cost in Alliance-affiliated factories (Management Survey 2017–2018). Despite some differences between these two initiatives, they served very similar functions: inspection of fire, electric and structural safety of factory; safety training to workers and management; and publication of progress reports (Labowitz and Bauman-Pauly, 2014). The similarities include a common set of standards based on the Bangladesh National Building Code, a common reporting template, mutual recognition of audits in factories that are covered by both A&A brands, safety training for workers and management, and publication of progress reports on each of their websites (Management Survey 2017–2018[1]).

6.2 Management experiences of Accord and Alliance

The managements' experience of Accord and Alliance (AA) was based on two methods: Key Informant Interviews (KII) and a survey. The participants of KII were senior staff of the Accord, a government employee from the Department of Inspection for Factories and Establishment (DIFE), a member from the ILO RMG project in Bangladesh, and the former Secretary of the Ministry of Labour and Employment. The research relies primarily on a survey of senior managers of 152 factories. For the analysis of this chapter, only AA-affiliated factories were used comprising senior management of 109 factories. The survey was conducted in 2017–2018. Among the factories, 67 was affiliation with Accord only, 15

Alliance only and 27 both Accord and Alliance. A snowball approach was used to get access to garment factories, by solely relying on the social network. The factories were diverse in terms of location and size. They were located in five districts – Dhaka, Narayangang, Gazipur, Savar, Chottogram. "Senior manager" here refers to Owner, Director, Managing Director, Human Resource Manager, Chief Accountant, and Compliance Manager. This section argues that although there have been significant breakthroughs in terms of developing a culture of safety adhered to by the government and entrepreneurs, the suppliers have encountered difficulties in implementing these initiatives. The limited support from buyers has posed a major challenge for the sustainability of this governance mechanism.

6.2.1 Paradigm shift on workplace safety

Until the inception of AA in 2013, the main concern of various stakeholders interested in CSR in Bangladesh was social compliance. Neither buyers nor suppliers were particularly concerned with the fire, electrical, and structural safety of factory buildings (Huq et al., 2016). The majority of the factory owners did not have any idea about how to ensure the safety of their buildings. Moreover, the building regulations which had been developed in the past 20 years had not been implemented adequately (Sobhan, 2014). The inception of AA is seen as a "breakthrough" since it is the first multi-stakeholder agreement that engages buyers to be committed to ensuring workplace safety in an effective way (Hensler and Blasi, 2013). It is a promising and unique initiative to enforce labour rights in the global apparel chain (Khan and Wichterich, 2015). The Accord presents an international framework combining the mixed role of public and private agencies in collaboration with other relevant stakeholders. Ryan (2013) praised the Accord as a "game-changer" because of the involvement of trade unions and labour rights campaign groups in a legally binding agreement. The formation of the AA represents an unprecedented collaboration among global brands to address the safety of factory building for the first time in the history of the Bangladesh garment industry (Labowitz and Bauman-Pauly, 2014).

The factory management who participated in this study also agree with the researchers on the positive impact of the AA on factory building safety. The management survey finds that the overwhelming majority (81%) of factory managers said that the most important change in the industry since Rana Plaza was the safety improvement. This was straightforwardly acknowledged by one of the managers: "It is a lesson for us. Accord/Alliance taught us how to improve and maintain standards." A major positive impact of the AA, therefore, has been the education of managers in modern technology and practices relating to the safety of buildings and workers, and the use of modern technology, such as Auto Fire-off Ball extinguishers, in addition to normal fire extinguishers, fire hydrants, fire doors, automated fire alarms and detection systems, DEA, central detection processes, automated sprinkler systems, etc. According to the ILO representative, while it is difficult to say that this attention to safety exists throughout the entire industry, it can be said with confidence that it exists in large factories.

The implementation of AA instituted the practice of transparency in the compliance process. These initiatives put pressure on suppliers to comply with the existing law of the country as spelled out in the Bangladesh National Building Code (BNBC). The inspection system differs from previous audits in several ways. The inspection team under AA visits factories; examines the fire, electrical and structural condition of the buildings; and draws up a CAP for the management to implement within a prescribed time frame; later, they follow up on this process.[2] The compliance report of each factory is published on the website so that the current status of the factory concerning the CAP is publicly available.[3] It is possible to know whether or not the factory is terminated or approved by AA. This is a far more transparent process than that associated with pre-Rana Plaza initiatives. Different stakeholders are now in a position to scrutinize the compliance report produced by the AA.[4]

According to the senior staff of Accord, the institution of a transparent compliance system has enhanced the competitive advantage of the Bangladeshi RMG sector: 'I think it's a competitive advantage because the Bangladeshi manufacturers can say that we are the safest garments industry in the world'. In line with this, suppliers appreciate that the AA has been successful in making sure that buyers continue their business with Bangladeshi garment entrepreneurs. There was a real fear that buyers would leave Bangladesh after the Rana Plaza disaster. As one of the senior staff of DIFE stated:

> The buyers made it clear if the government does not take any step to improve the situation, they will not work with any Bangladeshi company anymore. Bangladesh also had to assure the buyers that this type of event would not occur in the future. All the stakeholders in Bangladesh including the government were afraid of losing buyers. We were able to assure them by agreeing to Accord and Alliance.[5]

Correspondingly, the export earnings from RMG increased from US$24.49 billion in 2013–2014 to $29.2 billion in 2017–2018 (BGMEA 2020). The monitoring of factories by the AA inspectors has helped to some extent in achieving such growth rates during a turbulent situation.[6] It has become a key requirement of the buyers to place orders with Bangladeshi suppliers. Sixty-one percent of respondents opined that participation in the AA has been valuable for their factory perspective. Their participation in the AA became essential since the continuation of orders from buyers now depended on certification of factories by the AA. According to the Director of a garment company: 'Fire, electric and structural safety was not my concern at all, even my buyers never checked this, but after Rana Plaza, you can't get an order without getting approval from Accord/Alliance on building safety.' This highlights the difference from the traditional compliance regime where suppliers had little incentive to comply, but now under the AA, suppliers perceive compliance with safety standards as a necessity.

After the collapse of Rana Plaza, there has been a revolutionary change in the factory to ensure workers' safety. For the last few years, factory buildings have undergone intensive refurbishment and renovation. Fire doors and other firefighting appendages have been installed, while fire drills and audit inspections have regularly taken place in the factory premises. At present, the factory is quite safe against likely calamities or accidents. Adequate doors, as well as staircases, are provided to aid quick exit, routes are not blocked by storage materials, machine layout is well planned with proper signage for an escape route. These changes have created a realization in workers about the level of safety at their workplaces. Workers refuse to enter factories with even minor non-structural cracks. After the efforts of AA workers feel safe to work in a factory compared to the past since it is now mandatory to maintain safety is now mandatory to maintain in all the factories. As a result, workers can work in a calm and sound atmosphere, pouring attention into their tasks.

A leading garment owner's view on transnational governance sum up the overall impact in the following way:

> Rana Plaza was a tragedy for the whole nation. But tragedies help people to rectify their mistakes and to come out with a strong one. RMG sector has paid heavily for the Rana Plaza tragedy and also is rectifying assiduously and heavily but yet its exuberance is not enough. It's true that If Accor/Alliance had not been there, the poignant pressure would not have been created on the owners. If Accord and Alliance were not there, in that case, owners perhaps unified and of course, it would generate positive responses. But because of the prescribed remediation that Accord/Alliance provided for owners made it quicker to react quickly. Standards were all set and laid down before the owners in an arranged and orderly way, so it was very convenient to follow those guidelines. Accord/Alliance never did harass the owners but to put the thing incorrect way intense pressure was indispensable and must be created. They never did harass the owners but the pressure that they created was very excruciating and agonizing. The level of pressure was to an extent that sometimes owners wanted to give it up and desist. The practice of public shaming was inaugurated by Accord/Alliance. However, this pressure could not last for long. The buyers for whom owners did all those were unlikely to forsake this industry neither did they increase the price of products.
>
> (Management survey 2017–2018)

This statement leads us to the challenges the factory owners negotiated in dealing with the AA and it is presented in the following sections.

6.2.2 Discontent with the regulation process

While acknowledging the progress made as a result of the AA initiatives, managers also spoke of the negative aspects of the regulation process especially the inspection mechanism. The management survey reveals that 45% of the factory managers were not happy with the inspection process while 17% reported mixed reactions. Managers found it difficult to deal with multiple inspections by multiple inspectors who had little coordination between them. For example, one inspection team was satisfied with a particular structural issue, but the follow-up team included that issue as part of its CAP. Some aspect of engineering was considered to be a problem for one factory but highlighted as a problem for another. A first inspection team suggested a particular location for the fire door, but the second team disagreed and required this location to be changed. One of the owners said:

> In my factory, there was a water reservoir of 150000-liter capacity approved by my lead buyer. The Accord did not raise any objection about the capacity of that tank, but the Alliance recently recommended increasing the capacity to 300000 liters. Almost 1.50 crore taka [0.18 million USD] is being spent to increase the capacity of the tank.

Miscommunications in the inspection process led to wasted expenditures on the part of managers. For instance, this research found that the purchase of fire doors not certified by the AA led two factories to lose US$300,000. Some factories already had fire doors approved by their buyers, but since those doors did not fulfill the standard set up by the AA, the suppliers had to replace them with the certified doors. Factories have also experienced shortages of their engineers because, before the AA, provision for regular engineers was not necessary. Hence, managers struggled to understand some of the technical instructions given to them by the AA since they did not have engineers among their staff.

One of the problems of traditional CSR for management is the absence of a unified code of conduct. A similar problem arose at the initial stage of AA where both parties did not accept each other's inspection reports. If a supplier was inspected by both AA, a given issue was addressed differently. Later management raised this problem and the AA started to use the same inspection module. This meant that both initiatives adhered to the same inspection guide, and accepted the report of the other initiative's CAPs, allowing suppliers to benefit from a unified code of conduct on building safety. Such a unified code of conduct is missing in traditional CSR. Managers saw this as a way in which the AA improved on traditional CSR.

Nevertheless, many managers were critical of the organization of the inspection process. They would have preferred the same inspection team to have been in charge of the same factory throughout the process – from the first inspection to the last. However, the Accord disagreed with the issues raised by the management, believing them to be 'without merit,' according to a senior member of Accord. It was Accord's view that they have invested millions of dollars to train their engineers who have university degrees, and have worked with the international firms to enhance their professional development skills. To prevent corruption and reduce the influence of factory management concerning inspectors, the Accord intentionally sent different inspection teams at different times to the same factory. Two reasons for the increasing number of CAPs per factory were: the inability of inspectors to inspect large factories within one inspection and the dynamic nature of health and safety at workplaces. The first inspection covered the acute danger of building safety, and the follow-up inspection focussed on the remaining issues. Since factories frequently add lines, machines, electrical connections, distribution panels, etc., they require several inspections. According to the Accord "...although they don't want to demotivate factories... while there are new findings they need to be corrected."

Apart from the inspection process, another challenge managers encountered was to complete the CAPs in time. One-third of the sample factories' remediation status was "behind schedule" The management argued that the time frame given by AA was very limited. Many other issues should be taken into consideration: for example, the factories needed consultants, suppliers, and labourers. But AA did not consider these issues. For instance, there were some phases of retrofitting. At first, a standard plan had to be submitted to AA; second, a third-party consultant was appointed, who would assess the factory and this assessment report would be submitted to AA. If AA accepted the assessment report, the owners could apply for permission for retrofitting. After getting the permission, retrofitting construction was carried on under the supervision of a third-party consultant. AA also fixed a deadline to complete the retrofitting. Sometimes they gave two or three months and in some cases, they gave four months. Time was contingent on the amount of work required to be retrofitted. Sometimes it was not possible to complete the retrofitting within the given time. AA started the countdown immediately after issuing the approval. It took some time for the report to arrive at the owners, to negotiate with the engineers, to get the raw materials for retrofitting but AA did not consider these time-consuming issues. As a result, practically it was not possible to complete the tasks within the stipulated time. AA were unreasonably pernickety and unnecessarily procrastinate on some processes as stated by the management.

However, the Accord did not agree with managements' logic on a delay of remediation. According to an Accord representative,

> The biggest obstacle to the remediation getting completed is the factories are delaying in doing the remediation. They spend a lot of time coming up with a million different reasons. I don't know why they can't do it. And the reality is they can.[7]

On the other hand, managers argue that there are several practical issues that have not been taken into account as legitimate reasons for the delay: orientation towards the new system, complications in retrofitting, bureaucratic process, weak port facilities and resulting delay in receiving safety equipment in time, and scarcity of reputed consultation firms to do DEA.[8] The inspection process of AA had been designed in a way that frustrated the senior management of garments factories. According to management interviews, one inspection team was satisfied with a certain aspect of some structural issue but the follow-up team included the same issue in CAPs. Whereas one engineering issue was not a problem at all for one factory it was pointed out as a major problem in another factory. One of the garment owners said that a fire door was installed at different locations at different times in his factory. The first inspection team made a suggestion to management but the second inspection team overruled that suggestion. The inspection team was not efficient and often failed to provide a fair judgement of the CAPs to the respective factory. According to a respondent, different inspection teams visited the factory at different times and generated contradictory feedback. For instance, a group of inspectors from Alliance concluded that everything was okay except for some minor faults and recommended work on those identified faults. After three months another inspector team of Alliance found some major faults in the same factory. So Alliance's inspection reports are paradoxical. The respondent told the inspectors that in the previous inspections no objections were raised over these issues. In reply the inspector said it was not their business to ponder over who had inspected beforehand and what feedback they had come up with.

The garment owners believe that the inspection plan had not been organized and structured properly. It could be better for them if the same inspection team had been in charge of a particular factory. All throughout the process – from the first inspection to last – one inspection team needs to be engaged in the same factory. But in reality, according to the managements' view, the inspection team was different at different times of inspection. As a result, the first team came up with a list of CAPs and the follow-up teams handed over new lists of CAPs. One team identified the problems and another team reviewed the process. Questions were raised not only about the increasing number of CAPs but also about the entire process. The owners' community would be benefitted if the AA engineering team informed the owners of the problems of the factory in the first inspection. It might be helpful for the factory management to get the whole picture of their factory in terms of building safety and start fixing the problems in an organized way. But it never happened.

There was also issue of unilateral decision made by the Accord. For instance, a factory was inspected for fire, electrical and structural safety by Accord in 2014. According to Accord, after many attempts by the Accord staff the factory failed to submit a DEA and make adequate overall CAP implementation progress. The failure to cooperate prompted the implementation of a notice and warning process. Despite this notice and warning process, as stated by Accord, the factory owner continued to fail to implement the Accord CAP. The Accord signatory companies using this factory were therefore required to terminate their business relationship with this supplier. On the contrary, the owner of the factory which was terminated does not agree with the statement of Accord. According to the owner, after the submission of DEA, the Accord team after its first visit gave the building a green signal. But the second team raised some new issues on fire, electricity, and structural issues of the factory. The owner decided to shift to a new set-up, but it was delayed by eight months because of legal complications on the land where new factory was supposed to be built. The owner asked the buyers to give him some time while they sorted out the paperwork and worked on the fire safety of the old building. But the buyers in spite of having 20 years of relationship stopped the order. The owner could not work on the CAPs since it required huge financial investment, but without orders from buyers he did not have sufficient money to work on those CAPs. Meanwhile the factory owner arranged Tk. 50 lacs after selling some assets and tried to fix the CAPs on a building that they were about to leave in six months. The process expired by the time frame set by Accord. After that, Accord sent a warning letter to the company and claimed that they sat with the owner before sending the termination letter. However, the owner did not receive the aforementioned letter. Finally, Accord sent the owner an email to which he replied but did not receive a reply from Accord in return. The owner believes that Accord terminated the factories without following the formal process.

In another case, the factory was in a shared building but the owner was in no doubt regarding the strength of the building. It was built by engineers from Karachi and there was not a single crack in the building as stated by the owner. Alliance sent an inspection team and they said structurally the building was weak and had limited strength to accommodate a factory. They appointed a Bangladeshi engineering consultancy firm who completed DEA and fixed the problems and for 15 days all lines were closed. But Alliance was not satisfied with the consultancy firm's work. This consultancy firm could not stand up to Alliance's objection; whatever the engineering team of Alliance was saying to the factory appointed consultancy agency, that firm agreed with Alliance although the owner was confident of the structural strength of the building. Later Alliance rejected approval of the factory. The eighteen-year relationship with this buyer ended after Alliance's rejection. At that time the owner did not have any money to move to a new set-up. Finding no other alternative he decided to close the factory.

All workers and staff were disappointed and cried. Then the owner's engineer friend saw the DEA of the factory and also inspected his factory. The engineer did not find any fault with the building. The owner later challenged Alliance's decision, and the case was sent to a review team comprised of BUET, Alliance, and BGMEA. The BUET engineers found that the engineers of the Alliance team did not find the presence of a pillar on one side of the building, but it was actually there mixed in with a wall. After the meeting Alliance decided to withdraw rejection. It seemed to grant a new life to the owner as he said, "but it appeared as an insulting matter to Alliance. They looked for revenge." They gave the owner two days' notice to install a fire door in the main entrance. But the building was shared, the factory owner had to convince the owner of the building as well as all occupants of that building to install a fire door in the main entrance. Alliance did not give him that time. After two days Alliance rejected approval of his factory, which had started its journey more than a decade ago.

Relocation was another major challenge that managers experienced in the process of implementation. The majority of the factory owners, in particular of small and to some extent medium enterprises, do not own their factory buildings. This constituted almost all of the small factories in our sample run on rented floors of multipurpose buildings. Many issues of safety, ranging from the electrical installation to the fire escape routes, fire, and smoke compartments to smoke doors, do not lie within the purview of the factory owner, but of the building owner. Many of these buildings were not designed to be garment factories. So often times, it becomes difficult to fix the financial terms regarding those CAP measures that are relevant to the safety of the entire building with the owner of the building and other factory owners.

The setting up of the Review Panel by the Ministry of Labour and Employment extended an opportunity to the garment owners to challenge the decision of the inspection teams. For instance, in this research, one of the factories nearly lost a buyer after 18 years of business when the Alliance failed to approve it. The owner challenged Alliance's decision and the case was sent to the Review Panel who later found that the assessment to be wrong.[9] After participating in a meeting, the Alliance withdrew their rejection decision. It seemed to grant a new life to the owner. Having a Review Panel allows a space to justify the closure decision of the inspection teams. In addition to the Review Panel, the steering committee of the transnational agencies meets with BGMEA every six weeks to deal with any problems the suppliers have encountered during inspection and remediation.

Because of AAs, factories' operations had been hampered. While some of the remediating constructions could be undertaken while the factories were operative some factories had to be closed down as they were situated in shared buildings. This research found that some large garment companies had factories both in their building and shared or rented buildings. The workers in the rented building shifted to the company's factory building due to the shutting down of the operation of factories in the rented buildings. Transport was provided for the workers since the new workplace was quite far away from the previous workplace. The factory management started two shifts in their building to accommodate the migrant workers. As the factories operated in two shifts, the workers of each shift could not work for more than 8 hours. It meant there was no scope for the workers to work extra hours and no way to receive overtime pay. If the garment workers do not get the opportunity to work overtime they usually don't stay in that factory. Knowing this character of the workers, the management had to recompense the workers by paying wages for an extra 2 hours although they did not work overtime. Besides within the regular 8 hours, lunchtime is allocated 1 hour. This means the owner paid wages for 10 hours but got the service of 7 hours from a worker. The additional cost on workers continued until the construction of the new factory. Another company built up a new factory closing down the old one which was in the city. The workers of the closed factory started working in the new factory which was far away from their homes. Every day the company buses picked up the workers from their homes and dropped them after work in their homes. The commute took 4 hours a day. The company had to pay wages for 4 hours to the workers, which cost the company extra money. Moreover some workers had motion sickness; travelling made them nauseous, which hurt their level of production.

6.3 Asymmetric power relation

Without getting approval from AA it became difficult for the garment companies to survive. Buyers are abundant, but they would squeeze the owners if they found any infringement on compliance. Most of these factories were established 10/20 years ago and no thought was given to structural, fire, and electrical safety of the factory building. After Rana Plaza, the inspection approach by AA was launched within a short time but the owners did not plan to arrange money to remediate their factories. According to an owner:

> After 2013 I am struggling to sustain in this sector. There is no flow of order. I have to pay my workers. But there is no money with me. I am confused about whether to shut the factory down or to invest money on compliance issues. I want to keep hanging on.

Immediate after Rana Plaza, one of the leading buyers of the U.S., in a factory, told the owner to replace the existing doors of the factories. The owner imported the buyer's specified doors from China to the factory. But recently Alliance raised objections against these doors and recommended to take down the doors. In total 108 doors had to be taken down. All the money spent on those doors, specified by the buyer, went in vain. The owner drew the attention of the buyer in this regard and the buyer said that the mistake had been done inadvertently and pledged the owner that indemnification would be granted in the form of order placement. The respondent had asked the buyer to increase the price but they refused to do so. It was a huge loss for the garment owner but no compensation was provided.

At the initial stage of the journey of AA, both the buyers and AA put pressure to install the fire door but there was no clear instruction of any standards of fire doors. A few large garment companies showed their proactiveness by purchasing the fire doors as soon as possible. But after a while, they were informed by AA to get those fire doors that are Underwriters Laboratories (UL) certified but the owners already installed fire doors which were not UL certified. For instance, an owner bought 150 fire doors, and each of those cost US$1,000, a waste of $150,000.

As shown above, suppliers had to adapt to the new system. They had to undergo an unprecedentedly rigorous inspection system with public sharing of the extent to which they have complied with the rules and regulations required by these new governance approaches. Despite the Accord being billed as a model of shared responsibility, suppliers claim that the challenges that they faced could have been minimized with more support from the buyers.

The arrangement of funds to implement the CAPs has turned out to be the most challenging task for the supplier factories (Khan and Wichterich, 2015). Factories have responded proactively to implement low-cost CAPs and other easily manageable tasks, such as removing blockages from stairs or exit paths, fixing missing bolts, etc. But they have found it harder to implement the expensive CAP measures that include the DEA of the factory, sprinkler systems, and modern fire alarms with automatic smoke detectors (Khan and Wichterich, 2015). Having said this, large factories have generally been able to implement the suggestions provided by the inspectors. This allows them to demonstrate their financial capacity and commitment to buyers who are very big in the global market. Smaller factories, however, have faced major challenges in doing so.

The absence of a transparent system for financing remediation is a major drawback to multi-stakeholder initiatives: it allows any firm obligation on the part of buyers to support suppliers in fulfilling CAPs, to remain out of view (Labowitz and Bauman-Pauly, 2014). Factory owners express their frustration with the agreements according to which: ‘each factory is subject to separate, voluntary funding terms depending on their arrangements with individual brands and retailers’ (Labowitz and Bauman-Pauly, 2014). It was the expectation of the Bangladeshi suppliers, that the buyers would share the financial responsibility for the CAPs. According to a Bangladeshi garment entrepreneur:

> Everything that Accord has done is worthy of applause. I do not have any dissent with Accord in any way. But I hold resent the buyers for their insensitivity to the suppliers’ problems and for their reluctance

> to share the costs of complying with Accord requirements. The buyers have never come forward to help me with compliance issues. They always say it is your problem, not mine. They do not advance us loans to carry out the CAPS or even commit to giving us guaranteed orders.

Not a single factory in this study received financial assistance from buyers. One of the garment factory owners shared his experience of the financial demands associated with CAPs:

> I need 60 lac taka [71428.5 USD] to fix the factory to be compliant, [I] can't make any arrangement. Last four months I lost 32 lac taka [38095.3 USD] due to not getting adequate orders, also 3.5 crore taka [416666.67 USD] is my liability. If my factory is compliant I would continue good business, but I can't afford to be compliant. If I get money from the bank as a soft loan I will survive. I am thinking to shift factory but still where will I get the money?

In principle, there are provisions for the buyers to provide support to suppliers. According to article 22 of Accord, the responsibilities of the signatory companies include: (a) improve cash flow by reducing payment terms or prepaying orders; (b) increase revenue by guaranteeing orders for a longer period and/or for higher volume, and increasing price per unit and (c) inject capital: through joint investment, providing or guaranteeing loans, accessing donor or government support, or paying for renovations directly. But factory managers say that they have not received any support from buyers in terms of advance payment of orders so that they could use this fund for remediation. The financial assistance formed by other agencies such as the IFC was not much use. As explained by the ILO (2016: 3):

> Until recently, there were no financial products specifically available to the RMG sector for remediation. Factory owners faced a long bureaucratic loan application process and could only accept available term loans with high-interest rates. Interest rates for loans in local currency can range from 11 per cent to 18 per cent. One significant disadvantage for many factories is their inability to present proper, reliable audited financials to banks; this has a direct effect on the amount of collateral requested by financial institutions to guarantee the loan.

There has also been no attempt on the part of buyers to provide fair prices for the products of their suppliers, given the special circumstances. Although the orders have continued, the price of buyers decreased. Between 2012 and 2016, three of the five highest-ranking Bangladesh export revenue garment categories experienced a substantial price reduction of around 28.7% (International Trade Statistics Yearbook, 2017). According to an owner 'Prices should be higher to allow for the cost of compliance. But this is not happening. Instead, price is going down." This situation has been summarized by Scheper (2017: 1082):

> The achievement of the Accord here lies in the buying firms' agreement to take co-responsibility in assisting their 'ethically deficient' suppliers in implementing standards according to the corrective action plans. But the terms of this co-responsibility rely on the unequal relationship between buyer and supplier and the smooth flow of production relationship. The main burden remains with the supplier.

The AA is supposed to be based on shared responsibility, but sharing of financial assistance for remediation by buyers, and support for the garment sector to continue to be commercially viable appears to be missing from this understanding.

The garment owners who could afford to fix the CAPs are relieved but the journey was not smooth, they had to argue with the Accord engineering team on many issues. They were scared that if they got upset inspection team will write anything in their report. Then the garment owners will be in trouble. AA has the power to decide whether they would want to work with them or not and the Bangladeshi suppliers do not want a negative response from them that can damage the reputation of their garment companies. So they have compromised with the situation. Everyone is petrified in fear of AA who hold complete sway over the owners and the buyer takes advantage of this situation. According to an owner,

> There were some CAPs that are not related to safety at all from our understanding. But Accord said it needs to be fixed. What will I do? I didn't have any choice, can't argue. If I do the list of CAPs will be longer. Since the inspection engineer team understands their report is a very powerful weapon to control these big businessmen, they have misused that power. We do not want to put investment of millions of dollars at stake.

However, the garment owners believe that relationships with buyers as well as AA should be more flexible and based on respect for each other. Thinking of the future business, the factory owners have given them the unchecked privilege to remain obstinate and stick to their decisions at the negotiation table. Buyers could also easily repeal orders and turn towards other factories. This waywardness of the buyers has made the owners severely vulnerable to low prices and other problems. There has been an absence of confidence among the Bangladeshi suppliers that they have the ground to clamour for the fair action by AA without being the misgiving that buyers would abandon them. The Bangladeshi suppliers also believe that they do not get equal treatment in the global market mainly after the rise of AA.

According to garment owners, inspections by AA only take place in Bangladesh. There are also garment companies in China, India, Vietnam, Myanmar, etc. But AA do not possess any ground there and buyers also do not pressure the suppliers. Many countries are also doing business with no compliant issues. But only the Bangladeshi garment entrepreneurs have been forced to be compliant by the buyers mainly due to the Rana Plaza. As a result, the cost of the product is higher than those countries that don't care about compliance. Even in China buyers will not get access to any garment factories. So the Bangladesh garment industry has become less competitive in the global market.

The discussion in this section shows that there has been an asymmetric power relationship between buyers and suppliers during the AA regime. The pressure to reduce prices from the buyers continues, despite the significant investments of the suppliers in remediation. By concentrating the power of buyers through lead firm collective action, the AA have arguably increased the power imbalance between buyers and suppliers. Suppliers have been forced to comply with new safety standards, but buyers have not made a financial contribution to this beyond paying for the inspections and administrative costs of the AA. These new transnational governance initiatives have crafted an opportunity for the buyers to widen their supreme authority over suppliers. In the past, global brands maintain their authority over their suppliers by imposing strict conditions mainly on cost, quality, and delivery times (Locke et al., 2009). Under AA, as we have shown, suppliers realize that there is 'no escape' from safety compliances although they have raised questions about the inspection modality. The power imbalance makes them fearful of challenging the AA inspectors. From a safety perspective, this is desirable, but on the other hand, the lead firms have made a marginal contribution to the improvements, while the suppliers have been forced to redistribute money from profits to workers' safety. We call this "coercive compliance." As Scheper (2017) argues, this enhanced ability to influence suppliers does not derive from the legal status of the Accord, but rather from the inter-firm cooperation it entails. This article illustrates that this coordination facilitates a huge increase in the power of lead firms over suppliers. By exercising "coercive compliance" the AA has increased costs for suppliers, possibly rendering many smaller operations non-viable in the long term. This has not been compensated for by any financial contribution from lead firms to the expenses entailed in remediation.

To ensure continued business with the buyers, the suppliers did not have any alternative but to remediate their factories as instructed by the inspectors of the AA. Because of the institutional experimentation nature of governance (Reinecke and Donaghey, 2017), the governing body of the AA and the suppliers have been learning from every step of execution – an approach known as 'learning by doing' (Reinecke and Donaghey, 2017). However, the management expected a greater responsibility from the buyers to adapt to the changes in the global supply chain. We explain the paradox that on the one hand, the AA are perceived by local managers as saving the Bangladesh RMG industry after Rana Plaza, but, on the other, the BGMEA is now keen for the Accord to be excluded from the country. Improving safety standards saved the reputation of the industry at a crisis moment but later the management was dissatisfied with some of the processes of inspection and remediation. Although the buyers have kept their promise to continue to do business with the Bangladesh suppliers by giving orders, the entrepreneurs struggled to implement CAPs without financial assistance from buyers. The large suppliers, because of their financial capacity, have been in a better position to comply with this transnational governance approach in comparison to the small, and to some extent the medium, suppliers. The buyers have paid for factory inspections but shifted the much larger cost of remediation onto the shoulder of the suppliers (Barrett et al., 2018). Had there been more cost-sharing rather than "coercive compliance," the hostility to the Accord might have been mitigated. The failure of buyers to assist suppliers led to the fact that the terms of co-responsibility rely on the unequal power relationship between buyers and suppliers; the main burden remains with the suppliers in the global supply chain (Scheper, 2017). The management's discontent on some issues of the inspection, frustration on adaptation with this new governance initiative, and most importantly the lack of cost-sharing means that managers on balance perceive the AA to be a burden and stood up against the extension of Accord. As noted above, a compromise on the future of the Accord has now been reached, but whether some of its key merits – rigour, independence, and enforcement – can be maintained is an open question.

Notes

1 The management survey was conducted in 2017–2018 as part of a research project. BRAC Institute of Governance and Development (BIGD) at BRAC University in collaboration with the London School of Economics, the University of New South Wales, the Freie University, the University of Gothenburg initiated a research titled, "Changes in the Governance of Garment Global Production Networks: Lead Firm, Supplier and Institutional Responses to the Rana Plaza Disaster." This three-year research project was funded by the Volkswagen Foundation with Wellcome Trust and Riksbanken Jubileumsfond as part of the Europe and Global Challenges Program.

2 Factories should be commended for their efforts to remediate all critical items listed in their Corrective Action Plans (CAP). Source: http://www.bangladeshworkersafety.org/factory/factory-cap-completion.

3 Please see the following link for availability of CAP for the Accord's affiliated factories. Source: http://accord.fairfactories.org/ffcweb/Web/ManageSuppliers/InspectionReportsEnglish.aspx/.

4 Such as government of Bangladesh, Department of Inspection for Factories and Establishments, BGMEA, ILO, Buyers and various countries.

5 Fieldwork 2017–2018

6 Bangladesh Government and BGMEA faced tremendous peer pressure and an image crisis emerged soon after the incident. Source: http://rmgbd.net/rmg-sector-overcome-the-imagecrisis-bgmea/.

7 Interview with a senior staff of Accord during management survey 2017–2018

8 A Detailed Engineering Assessment (DEA) is a detailed structural engineering investigation and reporting of a building structure. A DEA is necessary when there is insufficient information and documentation on the building structure to determine the safety of the structure. Source: https://dife.portal.gov.bd/sites/default/files/files/dife.portal.gov.bd/page/cdf085fa$_1$643$_4$4*e*9$_b$ *fce*$_4$86*d*88359*e*16/3.%20*DEA*%20*Guidance.pdf*.

9 The Bangladesh Ministry of Labour and Employment formulated a Review Panel in 2014 to assess recommendations for closure of factory buildings by inspection teams under the Alliance, Accord and National Initiative. The Review Panel is composed of engineers from the Alliance, BUET and the Accord, the Director General of the Department of Factories and Establishments from the Bangladesh Government, as well as representatives of BGMEA, BKMEA and IndustriALL.

7 Challenges of sustainability

The previous chapter has analyzed the impact of Accord and Alliance (AA) on the Bangladesh RMG industry as perceived by the management. It found that these two transnational initiatives have had a positive effect on factories in terms of structural, fire, and electric safety. The management has been able to understand how to maintain the safety of their factory buildings by working closely with AA. At the same time, they have faced some challenges in the process of remediation and the limited support from buyers, particularly the unavailability of financial assistance from buyers has made it difficult for the suppliers to implement the CAPs. Finding no alternative, the management has paid the cost of remediation from its sources. Since the approval of AA has become the determinant factor of getting orders from buyers, these two initiatives have created an opportunity for the buyers to extend their asymmetric power relationships with suppliers. Despite these drawbacks of this transnational governance, the Bangladesh RMG has regained the confidence of the global buyers that were under threat immediately after the Rana Plaza. It took some time for the Bangladesh garments industry to get back to business after the tragedy and the export earnings increased from $24.49 billion in 2013–2014 to $29.2 billion in 2017–2018 (BGMEA, 2020). Since then, more than a hundred programs have been introduced by the stakeholders for the sustainable growth of the industry. However, the pathway of business sustainability is not free from challenges. Four areas of challenges have been analyzed considering their level of importance in the industry: lower labour productivity in the sector, complications in audit and code of conduct, the continuous decline of prices offered by buyers, and the sustainability of upgrading initiatives. It can be argued that the purchasing practices and corporate business models of profit-generation have generated these challenges in the global supply chain. How the suppliers manage their factories may not be the main concern, but rather in the way in which powerful buyers use their sourcing strategies.

7.1 Low labour productivity

Labour productivity is one of the key economic indicators closely linked to economic growth, competitiveness, and living standards within an economy. In the case of one of the most labour-driven export sectors, industry experts indicate that lower labour productivity in the RMG sector – a lifeline for the Bangladesh economy – is one of the biggest challenges faced by this industry today. While the sector's growth remains healthy mainly driven by the cheap labour cost, there has been a serious concern over the low labour productivity compared with the competing countries. Whereas each garment worker accounts for $7,000 in export in Vietnam, the figure is closer to $5,300 in the Bangladesh RMG, some 30% lower (Woodruff, 2014). Bangladesh is the second-lowest in labour productivity – per hour productivity is $3.4 compared to $11.1 in China, $4.7 in Vietnam, and $15.9 in Sri Lanka (Financial Express, 2019). Based on a sample of 60 factories, Woodruff (2014) finds low average efficiency rates of around 45% in Bangladesh.

Achievement of labour productivity has always been a prime objective of this industry since lower productivity adds to increasing production costs. While prices of locally manufactured apparel items fell by 3.64% and 7.04%, respectively, in Europe and the U.S. (top RMG export markets for Bangladesh) between 2014 and 2018, production costs on the other hand increased by 30% during this period as reported by BGMEA (Financial Express, 2019). A total of 133 factories closed in 2019 due to higher production costs and non-compliance issues, resulting in 62,528 people losing their jobs (Textile Today, 2020). The productivity of labour also affects a factory's lead time – the total amount of time required for completing a product beginning from the date of receiving the order to the shipment of the goods to the customer. A survey conducted by the Bangladesh Institute of Bank Management found that approximately 66% of garments exported by local producers could not be shipped to the destination on time. This greatly threatens the competitiveness of Bangladesh in the global arena, as its main competitors (e.g. Vietnam) require a much shorter lead time – Vietnam takes approximately half the lead time that Bangladesh needs.

The existing literature shows that labour productivity can be increased by social upgrading CPD (2018), female supervisor training (Macchiavello, Rabbani Woodruff, 2015), structured management practices (Bloom et al., 2017), and better occupational safety and health (OSH) environment (Samaddar, 2016). CPD (2018) has attempted to establish a relationship between productivity and social upgrading in order to explore how social upgrading can affect productivity. Social upgrading refers to the improvement in employment, standard, and rights at work, social protection, and social dialogue. Productivity has been measured by sales/workers investigated against a social upgrading index. The study found that firms with greater than median social upgrading have higher production values on average, which, in turn, could lead to the conclusion that social upgrading can lead to higher sales generated through increased confidence of buyers. Macchiavello, Rabbani Woodruff (2015) on the other hand, explored a gender-based approach to productivity analysis. They evaluated the effectiveness of female supervisors by implementing a training programme for selected production line workers. Disagreeing with the established norms that males are more effective supervisors than females, the research showed that if proper training and incentives were offered, the performance of female supervisors in terms of productivity and efficiency catches up to that of male supervisors. However, Fukunishi (2014) reports a lack of motivation to develop a training culture in Bangladesh's RMG sector due to high labour turnover.

Bloom et al. (2017) investigated whether the use of more structured management practices, focusing on monitoring, targeting, and incentives, are correlated with firm performance, concluding heterogeneous but broadly positive results. Similarly, another study by Samaddar (2016) on OSH management revealed that there is a close and positive relationship between the productivity of workers and the working space environment, a result also supported by the Better Work Vietnam programme. The latter study finds that workers from factories with a better work environment reach the daily production target 40 minutes earlier. Similar evidence has also been found in other industries. One of the ways to increase productivity is process upgrading which means enhancing the efficiency of production by, for example, offering training to workers to improve their skills (Fukunishi, 2014).

In one of my research projects conducted in 2016–2018, the senior management of 152 factories was asked how productive their workers were compared to other factories.[1] The survey finds 43% of factories were more productive, and 57% of factories considered themselves less labour productivity as well as the same level of productivity over the period compared to other factories even after investing sufficient resources for the well-being of workers. The qualitative analysis reveals several factors related to labour productivity. These are:

- Structural drawbacks
- Motivation from factory policy towards workers
- Professionalism attitude of workers
- Relationship between workers and mid-level management
- Migration of workers
- Long-time buyers
- Management strategy

A certain level of education is required for the garment workers not only to be conscious of their rights but also to attain the skills required in today's factories. Without basic education sometimes they are not in the position to absorb the knowledge they receive from different pieces of training offered by the management, business association, government, and NGOs. The mean year of schooling of Bangladesh garment workers was 5.9, and only 16.9% of workers had completed grade 10 or above (Kabeer et al., 2020). Due to the lack of minimum education, the workers are unable to get the maximum out of the training offered by the management to develop their skills. The frustration of a factory owner is expressed in this way:

> Workers are almost ignorant, it is often difficult for them to have the benefits of training. We offer different services for them but they are not yet ready to use them because they don't have minimum education. We

are moving to automation and also to produce high-end complicated garments. For that, you need skilled workers but we have a limited supply of educated skilled workers.

Another owner said:

> We are investing a lot of money for the welfare of workers but the return from them is not satisfactory. It is the overall problem of the country since our level of education at the bottom is very poor. That's why we don't have an adequate supply of skilled labor.

The large garment companies are dealing with this deficiency by setting up a training centre at their factory premises but the majority of the factories are left behind without this facility.

Accepting this structural problem, the factory management has relied on compliant and welfare programmes as a tool to motivate workers to be productive. The management effort is to improve the working environment and take care of the safety of workers as per the Bangladesh Labor Act 2006 and the ILO convention. Apart from the basic compliant issues, different welfare programs are available in different workplaces, such as day care, health care service, subsidized grocery shopping, canteens, annual sports and cultural programmes, etc., which make the workers more committed to their jobs. Nevertheless, the key motivating factor for the workers, as stated by the management, is on-time salary. The workers are secured and mentally healthy in realizing the fact that within the first week of the month they are going to receive their salary. It helps them not only to organize their household expenditure properly but also to pay the house rent on time. Such an on-time payment of rent presents a better image to their landlords. Because of this image, in times of crisis, they even get support from the landlords and others. In this context, one of the senior management said:

> We ensure on-time monthly wages. This is one of the reasons workers feel safe and comfortable working here as they know when they are receiving their salary and they know very much that they will not receive a salary on a delayed date. So the worker can give their full attention to the work and factory get more productive output from them.

The offering of various incentives such as getting money for punctuality, additional festival bonus, payment for fulfilling the production target also inspire the workers to be more productive. The supervisor of a good factory has shared his experiences in this way:

> Workers get incentives such as *Hajira* (attendance) bonus that is a bonus based on workers' arrivals on time. Every worker gets Tk 50 as *Hajira* bonus by just punching their cards on their way in, so a worker can get up to Tk 1400 just from their arrival bonuses, while in other factories

> the maximum bonus they get for the entire month is only Tk 200 or so. There are other incentives such as the bonus for piece-rate workers, who get a 2 per cent bonus on the amount they earn.

It is also true that very few factories are financially strong and strategically effective to motivate the workers with different incentives so that a productive workforce would contribute to the growth of the company.

Another reason for lower labour productivity is culture. In some factories, workers are insincere and possess a sordid mentality. For example, as a manager shared,

> If a worker is producing 350 pieces per hour and another worker, just next to him/her is producing 200 pieces in an hour, the latter one would dissuade the previous one not to produce more than 200 pieces in an hour saying that those extra pieces would not do any good to him/her.

A majority of factory management claim that their workers do not have a professional mentality; as one of the managers argued, "Non-productive time is very high. The workers always try to be busy gossiping with each other. They have no idea of responsibilities." To some factories, their workers are careless, not serious about work, and not attentive, which leads to lower productivity as well as a higher rejection rate of products. This characteristic can be explained from a cultural point of view as, in general, a lack of aspiration is embedded in the culture of Bangladesh.

However, there is another way to explain a lack of professionalism and it is the migration tendency of workers. Migration is one of the crucial problems of the Bangladesh garment industry. Almost all factories are suffering from turnover rate – ranging from less than 5% in factoring with a good working environment to more than 10% in average factories. Due to the availability of limited skilled workers in the industry, efficient and experienced workers migrate to other factories. For the average workers, the presence of thousands of factories presents an option to switch if not satisfied with the employer. It mainly happens to factories that are not compliant and not in the position to offer more overtime opportunities to workers. For this migration tendency, labour productivity is lower since it is difficult to retain the workers, particularly skilled labourers, and sometimes it is a waste of resources for the management. After investing in training, the management finds these trained workers move to another factory for a better salary with this upgraded skill. Few factories are productive because the same workers are working for a long time, so they understand the process and system. The migration problem is explained in the following way by senior managements of few factories:

> They move easily from one factory to another, they don't care about the job, rather sometimes they threat the factory management that they will quit the job.

> Some minimum wage workers are leaving one job to another that pays only Tk. 100 more. The newly replaced worker may not be efficient like the previous one. The newer one takes time to be easy with the new system. For this productivity of the factory falls.
>
> Most of the workers are the ‘moving workers’- means move from one factory to another in search of better salary or benefits. Therefore, these workers lack technical capabilities and dedication and inclusion of these workers, you cannot expect to run the factory smoothly as per your will. And hence the reduction of a target, always lower than the average.
>
> We have observed that workers who are working for a long time are more productive. We can request the workers to work more or even for more overtime or during the crisis period. The workers in reciprocity could understand the owners’ crisis point and give their best. Therefore there is a strong correlation between the working length of the workers and the production capacity.

Despite these drawbacks, some factories have been able to be productive because of the management strategy. The way the factory layout is designed, what type of machinery is being used, how workers, mid-level management, and top management communicate including are all related to labour productivity. To reach the expected target, the operating management is monitored strictly along with maintaining operator skill test regularly. The engagement of the Industrial Engineering team has become a recent inclusion to ensure a planned process control system with upgraded machinery. Adequate resources are supplied to train mid-level management to reduce the gap between workers and managers. In some factories, the management maintains honest, frequent two-way communication between workers and managers, including constructive discussion of workplace issues. The workers are informed of the incentives and rewards across all departments so employees see the benefits of the effort. According to an owner, “The management always tries to decrease the distances and conflicts between the employees of all the departments as well as enhance the work efficiency of the workforce which eventually results in a high production.” Because of the differences in the skills of supervisors, there can be a variation in productive efficiency across production lines within the same factory. The workers try to do what middle-management exactly tells them to do. Since the staffs of middle-management come from different backgrounds and levels, each of them has a different attitude and mindset which has a different effect on productivity. Due to the traditional mentality of few managers and supervisor, for example, if the owner expects 100 products to be produced in an hour, the workers produce 80 products; for 20% deficiency the owner has to pay for overtime.

The last but not the least factor related to labour productivity is the relationship with buyers. From the management experiences, it is evident that productivity becomes higher when the factory has the same buyer for a long time. The advantage of having long-term buyers is that workers are familiar with their style and no need to change the factory layout frequently. Echoing this one of the owners mentioned:

> We used to carry orders for limited buyers and workers for the whole year tend to produce the same products. They were quite well known about the design and often, they can produce at their maximum speed. However, for the last three years, we are working for multiple buyers and even for the same buyers, the design has been changed. Due to the changed design, the same workers have to adopt different designs in a month. These make the production process slow as they were not used to do this type of work and subsequently these make delays of production.

Hence, workers tend to be less productive. Another entrepreneur said: "Generally workers are productive if they are producing one single product. However, once they produce different products at the same time, they become less productive." Buyers' sustainability is also related to productivity in terms of getting an order for the whole year. The long gap between orders disrupts the workflow and as a result, the workers don't have a workload all over the year. During the off-peak time, the workers remain less busy and the rhythm of work is lost.

Whatever the problems of enhancing labour productivity are, it is high time for the Bangladesh RMG to adapt to the changing nature of the global business model. For sustainable growth in the RMG industry, market experts have consistently emphasized the importance of labour productivity to achieve shorter lead times and competitive pricing. Because of frequent changes in the taste and affordability of consumers, the fast-fashion trend is growing in tandem with bulk orders. There has been a huge demand from the consumers to have the latest fashion quicker at a lower price leading to reduced time for the suppliers. The workers have to adapt fast, facing a steeper learning curve with the continuous changes of style, while trying to speed up production. In this fast-fashion model, labour productivity is an important part of the business to remain competitive in the global market.

7.2 Complexity of audit and codes of conduct

From diverse backgrounds, the Bangladeshi garment entrepreneurs started to invest in this industry by taking advantage of cheap labour and flourished with very limited labour surveillance (Uddin, 2008). Attempts at intergovernmental regulation through the addition of a social clause including the core labour standards of the ILO in the World Trade Organization (WTO) were not successful in the mid-1990s (Pahle, 2010). Anti-sweatshop activists, therefore, turned their attention from governments to high-profile garment brands, who responded by developing Codes of Conduct and joining multi-stakeholder initiatives (Bartley, 2007; Merk, 2011). Such codes frequently included ILO core labour standards (though sometimes omitted freedom of association and right to collective bargaining) and were subject to regular auditing by the lead firm and/or a third party. This wave of regulation through codes of conduct improved working conditions in the Bangladesh garment industry by removing child labour from the sector in the late 1990s as well as forming a welfare committee in the EPZ (Rahman, 2014).

Yet evidence suggests that buyers' codes of conduct produced limited results in other areas such as health and safety, working time and wages (Locke, 2013; Locke, Qin and Brause, 2007; Locke and Romis, 2006; Vogel, 2008). The traditional compliance model has numerous shortcomings as argued by Locke et al. (2009: 320). For example, auditors sometimes lack the skills required to conduct a thorough audit (Pruett et al., 2005). Audits may also be conducted by an agent of the buyer, which in turn creates an inherent conflict of interest (O'Rourke, 1997). The code system is especially weak in upholding workers' rights regarding trade union membership and collective bargaining (Anner, 2012; Barrientos Smith, 2007). Fundamentally, some commentators have argued that the codes are designed to limit legal liability rather than to improve labour standards (Esbenshade, 2004; Rodriguez-Garavito, 2005). Given the rarity of punishment, the incentives for suppliers to improve compliance have been weak (Locke et al., 2009).

In this context, a recent study by Reinecke et al. (2019) portrayed two cases of the failure of social audits to improve the safety of garment factories in Bangladesh. One factory inside the Rana Plaza had previously passed SA800 by an audit company named Bureau Veritas on behalf of a Canadian brand Joe Fresh (Reinecke et al., 2019). Another factor of this complex was audited by TUV Reheinland, and awarded Business Social Compliance Initiative (BSCI) certification. In the process of finding reasons behind the failure of the audits, Reinecke et al. (2019) identified critical weaknesses of CSR: (1) failure of codes of conduct to address systemic problems (2) failure of individual action to tackle systemic problems (3) hyper-flexibility and shifting of commercial risk to suppliers (4) lack of transparency (5) lack of integration of CSR in commercial purchasing decisions and strategy (6) failure of CSR to affect purchasing practices (7) lack of meaningful worker representation and (8) the implementation gap of Freedom of Association clauses in codes of conduct. In line with this, the implementation of the prevailing social audit is bedevilled by low-quality inspections, poor value for money, unnecessary duplication of audits, inconsistent CAPs, and audit fraud. A collective action by buyers to monitor and enforce codes of conduct is missing in practice, which leads to lower enforcement incentives from buyers and audit fatigue of suppliers (Reinecke et al., 2019). In some cases, CSR budgets are under-funded and CSR officers struggle to work together with the commercial team whose prime agenda is an aggressive price negotiation. Such tendencies squeeze the suppliers as is evident in the Global Survey on purchasing practices that 52% of suppliers in textile and clothing accepted orders below production cost (Reinecke et al., 2019).

The flaws of both governance approaches – public (weak institutions) and private (buyers' code of conduct) – was starkly demonstrated by the Rana Plaza tragedy in Bangladesh, and this paved the way for the emergence of another regulation. A need for "shared responsibility" and a multi-stakeholder approach has opened up opportunities to address responsible behaviour. Such a multi-stakeholder governance approach has been employed in the Bangladesh RMG, known as the Accord and the Alliance.

What is noticeable is several regulations – private and public – have been evolved. But, from a management perspective, a common problem of private regulation is the absence of a unified code of conduct. Our management survey (2017–2018) reveals that code surveillance appeared to be common in the Bangladesh RMG industry. On average each factory follows four codes and receives nine audit visits a year by a lead firm or third-party auditors. Besides, there are regular visits by the buyer's compliance staff who work closely with the supplier's compliance team to prevent violations of labour practices. Auditing regimes, comprising a mixture of lead firm and third-party auditors, have also tended to converge, with more emphasis on securing management agreement to improve factory audit scores over time rather than a "tick boxes" approach that demonstrates superficial compliance. The most common audit accreditation was BSCI (64% factories), followed by various categories of ISO (15%), WRAP (12%) SEDEX (6%), and OKOTEX (3% factories).[2] However, code implementation was not free from problems. The management suggests that although there is no significant variation of various codes, a unified code of conduct would make their lives much easier. The rationality of a unified code of conduct is evident in the following management experiences.[3]

> Most of the buyers do have similar kinds of requirements so we do not face problems often but there are some difficulties faced on overtime issues. The way one buyer code of conduct pays over time is different from another buyer. But we follow the rule of the current buyers to avoid complexity.
>
> One buyer asks for 8 hours per day working hours, another 10 hours considering Bangladesh's context.
>
> One certain buyer visited a factory and upon finding the first-aid box empty, they asked why it was empty. Some days later, another buyer came and found medicines in the first-aid box and grumbled on it because workers could have eaten the medicines. These sorts of dichotomy still exist. There should be a univocal code of conduct. Buyers want workers' safety, hazardless working conditions, and integrity. BGMEA has been asking the buyers to constitute a uniform code of conduct.

The absence of a unified code of conduct also leads to another problem. Over half (55%) of the respondents highlighted the time and effort required was difficult to manage. Often the factories are overburdened by the frequent visits of buyers' audit team and their level of involvement. A significant time and effort of the HR and compliance department of the factory are invested in preparing a document for the audit team. Different buyers come on different days and check the same issues with the presence of management. These audits require the continuous involvement of the compliance team. The experience of the audit is presented in the following box.

Box 7.1 Audit experience of a factory compliance manager

We have ten buyers currently, so on average we face an audit once a month based on the current matrix of the buyers. There are some other requirements as well. Along with audits they have environmental requirements on ETP, chemicals, SEDEX, BSCI, etc. Apart from these C&A will come with social audit, energy audit, technical audit, and what not! Our two lead buyers are H&M and C&A. H&M follows the Higg Index which covers all aspects including social, environmental along with AA issues. C&A has its auditing format. H&M audit is broader but it is at the same time easier for us too because we can answer the questions while providing supporting proof with that. There is no need for something like hiding and seek or any sort of gameplay. But for other buyers, it depends on the perception of the particular auditor. In that case, audit results get filtered through the personal belief of the auditor. The Higg Index is a public platform where some other buyers are on the same platform. Up to this year, they have been sending their auditors but the discussion is going on to send a third party from now. C&A send their internal team other than the development officers. They have two categories – one is for development, and the other is for audit. Higg is once a year, and C&A is every six months. For C&A, if the factory receives a "C," then the gap between two audits is six months; if a "B," it is one year; and if an "A," then it is two years. We are currently categorized as "C," but our position fluctuates between "B" and "C." As I said, there is fluctuation because the result of the audit depends on the perception of the auditor. But it is different in Higg. The questionnaire is already on the platform; we just have to answer the questions and submit them with proper documents to evaluate ourselves. Higg is better. Having the questionnaire means you have the scope for improvement and implementation and then you have to show the proof. For Higg, what matters is the implementation, not the format. Our factory's rating last year was "B+" (63–65%), for both social and environmental in Higg Index which can be interpreted as "above average" in the current Bangladesh context. But we got "C" in the C&A audit.

The sustainability of our efforts is the best outcome of audits. For example, the installation of fire safety equipment requires a huge investment. But if you do not concentrate on regular maintenance, then the whole investment will become useless. Now we know and the industry knows how to maintain because of the system we have implemented. The audit has an impact on productivity and product quality because if we can strictly maintain the housekeeping then efficiency will rise. Whatever parameters are used by the buyer, it will help in such improvement. For example, the monitoring process of the audit system helps you do the housekeeping properly and that results in an increment of quality. If you talk about overtime based on buyers' code of conduct when it is maintained then automatically the labourers become more productive, healthy, and capable of producing more products of higher quality. It has also an effect on the environment, for example, we're concerned about water. Water is also being saved because of this monitoring and control mechanism. We and almost all the other factories are implementing the rainwater harvesting method, which was a requirement of the buyers, especially H&M.

However, the main problem is that the codes of conduct are inconsistent. Different auditors ask different questions on the same thing. For example, a boiler operator's certificate is required. But on the same document, someone is providing B and another person gives C. It also varies with the change of buyer. Sometimes it becomes quite difficult to understand what documents they are asking for. We have to manage this problem. We include the issue into CAP, collect information, do research, and then implement that before the next audit. In my observation, this is kind of a business. Their mindset is not to let us go up because if we stay down, they can always come up with business; business from an auditing perspective. If they can find problems in my factory and if I get a low grade, then I have less bargaining power. There has been an impact of this inconsistent characteristic on productivity. This inconsistency leads to fluctuation in the order level. Because of the audit inconsistency, your actual production order will not match with the preliminary projection or forecast, and this will take down productivity. So, the buyers' audit system is inconsistent and that's why we should go for a unified code of conduct something like Higg Index. If all the buyers endorse the Higg Index, then we can fully concentrate on one set of requirements. You see, a huge requirement is also already pending for Higg because the factory got 66% so, there is still a 30–40% scope for improvement. See, having multiple codes means, first, variation in requirements. Second, you have to produce different sets of papers or documents. For example, if there is an injury report of the workers, then the management has to write the report in one format for one buyer and in another format for another buyer. So they have to take a double burden for a single task. Because of such duplication of works, productivity goes down. You can share the information with your buyer if you are somehow not satisfied with the auditor for his misbehaviour or misconduct. You can let the buyer know. But you know, there are reasons for which it is very difficult for us to do.

Source: Management survey 2017–2018.

7.3 Squeezing of prices

After the catastrophic Rana Plaza factory collapse, international scrutiny, and the threat of withdrawing investment from buyers and suspension of trade privileges by the U.S., forced the suppliers as well as the government to showcase a visibly constructive and proactive approach to secure workers' safety. The tension was explained by the former Secretary of Ministry of Labour and Employment of Bangladesh (Fieldwork, 2018) in this way: "The whole world grew hostile towards us. I felt we will not be able to supply garments to foreigners anymore. We were lucky. We welcomed the idea of Accord and Alliance wholeheartedly." In addition to allowing the AA to inspect the factories in the country, the government set up a National Initiative for factories that were not covered by these two transnational initiatives. The cost of compliance has been increased significantly to address the prescriptions of the AA as stated by one of the owners: "We spent 27 crores [$3.3 million] in the last few years to accomplish the demands of a proper compliance adhering factory."

On the contrary, as argued by Kabeer et al. (2020),

> Lead buyers continued to pursue purchasing practices that went directly against the financial feasibility of local suppliers. Not only did they fail to increase the procurement prices paid to local suppliers, one way to have offset some of the remediation/relocation costs incurred by the latter, but the prices they paid maintained their steady long-term decline.

The pressure to reduce prices from the buyers continues, despite the significant investments of the suppliers in remediation. According to Schüßler et al. (2019) only 12% of buyer's CSR managers agree to pay higher prices to suppliers for compliance measures (see Box 7.2). Although the orders have continued, the price of buyers decreased. Between 2012 and 2016, three of the five highest-ranking Bangladesh export revenue garment categories experienced a substantial price reduction of around 28.7% (International Trade Statistics Yearbook, 2017). Although the labour networks have successfully pressed the buyers to sign a legally binding agreement to inspect the factories of suppliers, this new transnational governance has not questioned the purchasing practices and corporate business models of profit-generation, which are the fundamental causes of non-compliance in the global supply chain (Scheper, 2017). Anner et al. (2013) support the view that the root cause of poor labour conditions is not how the suppliers manage compliance in their factories, but rather in the way in which powerful buyers use their sourcing strategies. By exploring the relationship between prices, what suppliers are paid to produce apparel, and the status of workers' rights in exporting countries, the authors found that the declining price which was paid by buyers has indirectly generated pressure on suppliers to adjust to the trend of quick shipment with a lower price by violating the internationally recognized labour standards. In his recent research, Anner (2018) finds evidence of corporate business models of generating profit. Based on a survey of 223 factories in Bangladesh, Anner's (2018) study shows that since the Rana Plaza incident, the price paid by buyers to suppliers has declined by 13% and lead time declined by 8.14% between 2011 and 2015. There was also a steady reduction in delivery times as is evident in Anner's (2018) study that in 2011, the major global brands gave factories in Bangladesh an average of 94 days to complete an order; by 2016, it had declined to 86 days, a decline of 8.14%. How the buyers have squeezed suppliers is also presented in Table 7.1. Our management survey 2017–2018 finds that the most challenging factor to maintain a compliant factory is not getting appreciation from buyers in terms of a better price. There has also been no attempt on the part of buyers to provide fair prices for the products of their suppliers, given the special circumstances. According to the management survey (2017–2018) a third (33%) of factories earned between 0 and 2% annual profit, and 38% earned between 2 and less than 5%, while only 24% of factories reported a profit of 5% or more. This finding is supported by Anner that shows the profit margins have been declining among Bangladesh suppliers by 13.3% between 2011 and 2016 leaving them with a mean profit margin of 7.69%. Comparing the past, a factory owner explains the current lower profit margin in the following statement during the fieldwork.

> The profit that the first generation owners made was an anomaly and beyond example in comparison with other businesses. But at present, this business has become competitive. Previously many factories did not pay wages to the workers regularly and some owners have migrated to Canada by dissipating money. But now these sorts of malpractices cannot be done. At present, it takes three times more money to make a factory than it took before. ARP (Air Raid Precautions) system has been installed everywhere to detect the spot from where the fire originates. There must be a daycare and doctor in the factories. Random and unnoticed audits have been conducted nowadays. There should be a canteen and entreating space for the workers. If an LC order is of $100000,

> 75 per cent of it is paid back to back on raw materials. Out of the reaming 25 per cent, government charge is 1 per cent as tax and overhead cost is 20–22 per cent. At last 3 per cent remains and this is profit which is gained after tremendous stress.

The vulnerability of suppliers regarding ethical price is also shared by other suppliers in the factory management survey.

> For us, price is the major difficult challenges. There is no rational adjustment between the quality and building compliance and price of the FoB i.e. the buyers are offering.
>
> Our cost escalated a lot due to workers' wages, meeting up the building compliances. However, their [buyers] price is decreasing day by day.
>
> On buyer's demand, we are investing a lot on compliance issues but they [buyers] are not willing to give a good price by which we might have to do a minimum profit. Now we are doing business for the sake of our factory and workers only because if the factory closed there will be huge unemployment.
>
> For each product, the buyer paid 5 pound dollars and sold it at 12.5 pounds in the market. After Brexit, the buyer curtailed the price to 10 pounds.

These experiences of suppliers regarding buyers' prices are not new at all. A study conducted in 2003 by Rahman (2014) also reflects similar findings. Moniruzzaman – former president of the BGMEA – outlines his views on the difficult situation in which garment companies find themselves in the following way.

> Our buyers focus on working conditions. But they don't give [an] ethical price in return for good practices in the workplace. Buyers demand good working conditions and other facilities. But they are not giving the right price. Those who say about ethical working condition, they should also speak about ethical price. If we upgrade the facilities we need money. If we get a good price we must follow ethics. But buyers don't compromise with price.

The garment manufacturers are vulnerable in the sense that they know if they cannot agree to low prices for their products (at the cost of low wages and adverse working conditions), the buyers relocate their sources of production. The manufacturers are well aware of the fact that they can push their workers by providing low wages or not paying wages on time, but the owners cannot force their buyers to increase the price of their products. This means that the garment employers do not have sufficient bargaining power concerning the buyers. Being unsuccessful in offering a low price for their garments leads to the loss of orders. It is not the case that the buyers are unaware of the workers' conditions: the buyers know how the workers are producing their orders. Consumers, human rights organizations, and other global institutions stress the point to buyers to be strict in complying with the code of conduct. As a result, buyers pressure owners to improve working conditions. But the question is: do the buyers want to eliminate the unhealthy working conditions that exist in the workplaces? This intention of buyers is also known to the trade unions as Amin argues that the lower profit margin is also the reason for the sufferings of the workers.

> You will also observe that the garment trade is global. The ultimate gainers are the multinational companies. Suppose they buy a denim shirt from us for $30–40 per dozen, whereas they sell each shirt for US$15–20. So imagine the profit. They buy T-shirts from here for $1 and sell it for $8–12. It means their profit is ten times higher. If the buyers offer a good price to us, I think the exploitation of the workers will be no more. We just want a reasonable price from them, not an unbalanced trade. Although we directly blame employers for bad situations, these buyers are responsible for the sufferings of the workers.

The fast-fashion business model and the consumer are also responsible for squeezing the prices. From the broader structural perspective, Taplin (2014) argues that the suppliers have come under greater pressure in the last decade as global brands and retailers embraced the "fast-fashion" business model. The rise of this new model, as the author claims, is the logical continuation of Lean Retaining (LR) and Quick Response (QR), and is designed to produce cheap fashionable items targeting young customers with income scarcity. In the regime of "fast fashion," western consumers have fuelled the demand for a greater variety of clothing every year at ever-cheaper prices. Instead of three seasons per year, the retailers have persuaded a change of fashion almost every month. As a result, "...retailers have reconfigured supply chains to facilitate speed and low-cost production; sub-contractors have aggressively competed with each other to gain valuable orders, and to do so, intensified work and depressed wages" (Taplin, 2014: 79). Surprisingly, the average western consumers are reluctant to pay more for the clothing and seem to be indifferent to altering their purchasing behaviour (Santoro, 2000; Tobin, 2013). This model has been successful and ultimately the suppliers have no other option than to deal with the low price offered by the buyers.

To some extent, the buyers are not only responsible for these purchasing practices. Some large factories in Bangladesh exercise unethical practices. In our management survey, a supplier gave an example of a 60-line factory. This factory sells the products of 20-line at a reasonable rate to buy the products of the remaining 40 lines are sold at a minimum rate. For this large factory, it is essential to run the factory all the time and at least to get the operational cost they agree to prices with no profit from buyers. As a result, small factories around this factory can't stand against it because it is a complaint factory and the buyer takes advantage of it. It means that the level of unity is very low among Bangladesh suppliers. If they were united, they would stand up together for unfair prices from the buyers. Greater collaboration among garment manufacturers is missing in the industry to prevent the exploitation of buyers on prices. The solidarity of suppliers is required not only from the local context but also from the global landscape since all suppliers have faced a global and common problem. Criticizing the 'divide and rule' approach of the global brands and retailers, Mostafiz Uddin (June 15, 2020) has raised some questions to think about for the global suppliers: "As garment manufacturers, can we not agree on some minimum acceptable standards that we all agree must be abided by from brands?"

Table 7.1 How often did the following situations occur in the factory?

Management response	*% often*	*% several times a year*
Buyer changed style after placing order	10.5	0.7
Buyer made an untimely increase in ordered quantity	17.1	9.9
Buyer requested shorter lead times	15.8	27.0
Factory accepts orders that exceed its production capacity	7.9	0
Brand sourcing and social compliance staff communicated contradictory information to factory	11.8	2.6
Factory fails to reach planned production levels	2.6	0.7
Problems with production equipment (e.g. needles break)	1.3	3.9
Limited ability to adapt capacity to fluctuating orders	4.6	3.3

Source: Schüßler et al. (2019).

Box 7.2 Buyer-supplier relationship: Buyer's CSR managers' response

68% of CSR managers have a veto right regarding new supplier selection
48% of CSR managers say their influence in the company has increased
58% of CSR managers state that the importance of CSR for corporate strategy is high or very high in their firms
12% of CSR managers agree to pay higher prices to suppliers for compliance measures
25% of firms in our sample directly support supplier upgrading initiatives

Source: Schüßler et al. (2019).

7.4 Sustainability of upgrading initiatives

The question of sustainability of the suppliers has become difficult when the compliance cost is going up, on the one hand, and the price offered by the buyers is going down. While the sector's growth remains healthy, there has been a serious concern over the sustainability of the Bangladesh RMG which depends on three areas: the increasing cost of compliance, squeezing of prices, and fast-fashion business model. The hyper-competitive structure of apparel global supply chains has contributed to a buyer-driven sourcing squeeze (Anner, 2018), and the structure that is dominating now is the fast-fashion business model. It is high time for the Bangladesh RMG to adapt to the changing nature of the global business model. For a long time, the apparel industry produced and ran clothes for four seasons a year, a model that offered sufficient time for the designers and other stakeholders to contribute. Because of the frequent change of taste and affordability of consumers also with the deeper intensification of globalization, the fast-fashion trend has replaced the previous model. There has been a huge demand from the consumers to have the latest fashion quicker at a lower price leading to compressed time for the suppliers. The workers have to adapt fast with the continuous changes of style and speed up the production. In this fast-fashion model, upgrading the factory is an important part of the business to remain competitive in the global market.

Traditionally, it was assumed that economic upgrading within the global value chains would bring social upgrading with it. Bernhardt and Milberg (2011) studied the relationship between economic and social upgrading using the available international dataset across sector and country wise in the global value chains. They defined economic upgrading as an increase in the world export market share and an increase in the export unit value. An increase in employment and real wages were two determinant factors of social upgrading. The finding showed variation in the relationship between economic and social upgrading. Although there was clear economic upgrading in the mobile sector, it leads to very little social upgrading. In the apparel sector, there appeared to have been a positive correlation but some countries went through social downgrading along with economic upgrading. From a country perspective, while Mexico maintained economic and social upgrading, India and China achieved significant economic upgrading at the cost of weak social upgrading. In sum, the evidence of Bernherdt and Milberg (2011) shows that economic upgrading does not translate automatically into social upgrading. From their extensive reviews of issues in this area, Barrientos et al. (2010) and Milberg and Winkler (2011) suggest that economic upgrading only sometimes translates into improvements for workers. The empirical evidence reveals that there appears to be a positive correlation between economic and social upgrading, but there are some examples where economic upgrading led to social downgrading (Bernhardt and Milberg, 2011). The institutional and policy conditions such as Aid for Trade could lead to a closer alignment of economic and social upgrading (Bernhardt and Milberg, 2011). The other factors that influence the relation of economic and social upgrading are particularities of specific industries, position within the global value chain, typology of labour, the status of workers, etc. (Salido and Bellhouse, 2016). The employee status could also be another factor since some studies have found that economic upgrading brings social benefits to permanent workers and social downgrading to irregular workers (Bernhardt and Milberg, 2011; Lee, Gereffi and Nathan, 2013; Rossi, 2013). The nature of governance as well as the sustainability policies of lead firms can also have a huge effect on the quality of life of workers at all levels of the value chain (Nathan and Sarkar, 2011; Rossi, 2013).

In the context of the Bangladesh RMG, the CPD's (2018) study assesses the capacity of apparel enterprises to undertake economic and social upgrading to be competitive in the global market. Upgrading levels of factories have been divided into three parts: economic upgrading, social upgrading, and gender embedded upgrading. Economic upgrading shows the advanced levels of firms in terms of productivity and technology; social upgrading shows the development of rights and entitlements of workers, while gender embedded upgrading shows how much of the upgrading has been gender-neutral. Three indexes were designed in the research. The firm's economic upgrading index was calculated from the weighted index of process, product, and functional upgrading sub-index. The social upgrading index was based on employment, standard, rights, and non-discrimination sub-index. Gender Embedded Index was measured from gender embedded employment, standard, rights, and non-discrimination sub-index. Based on a random sample of 193 factories and 2,270 workers, the CPD (2018) found that the overall score of the economic upgrading index was low. Large enterprises lead the economic upgrading because of their financial capacity as well as the capacity to take risks for introducing new technologies and innovation. The social upgrading score was high in most of the factories. Considerable improvement in social issues – improvement of employment, safety, and privileges of workers – was demonstrated. The performance of different firms in social upgrading was far better than the performance in economic upgrading. The overall performance of sample firms in gender embedded social upgrading was moderate. The analysis of the survey reveals that the relationship between price and upgradation was rather weak both in the case of economic and social upgrading. More importantly, the relationship between price and social upgrading was rather weaker than that of economic upgrading. The survey shows that there was no trend in the relationship between economic upgrading scores and profitability. With regards to social upgrading, there seems to be some indication that higher profitability has helped in higher levels of social upgrading, or, in other words, firms with better profitability have better social upgrading scores.

The following projects (Table 7.2) or supply chain initiatives have been brought into the Bangladesh RMG industry by different stakeholders

Table 7.2 Different upgrading projects in RMG

Projects	*Objectives*
• Better Work Bangladesh by ILO and IFC	• Improving the working conditions of the Bangladesh RMG
• Supplier Qualification Programme by GIZ	• Improve the living and working conditions of RMG workers
• Promoting Workplace Cooperation in the RMG Sector in Bangladesh by ILO	• Ensure and sustain harmonious industrial relations
• Promoting SRHR through Inclusive business in the Bangladesh Garments Industry by SNV	• Improve SRHR services at workplaces
• HER by BSR	• Women health, financial access
• Lactating Mother Allowance Programme	• Focus on pregnancy health care, safe motherhood, and mental development of children 0 to 5 years
• Episode-9 by BGMEA	
• Social Dialogue by ILO	• Sustainable improvement in social dialogue
• Essentials of OSH (EOSH)	• Training and awareness creating programs on OSH.
• Developing Capacity Building Framework for Green Industries by AFD	• Feasibility Study on Capacity-Building Framework for Green Industries.
• PaCT by IFC	• Environment, water, and energy efficiency
• Mapped in Bangladesh by C&A and BRAC University	• Digital mapping of factories
• SUDOKKHO and Sarathi by Swiss Contact	• Skill development and Financial Inclusion
• Skill for Employment Investment Program by ADB	• Skill development
• Gender Equality and Returns (GEAR) by ILO and IFC	• Get more women in supervisory roles
• Sweden Textile Water Initiative (STWI)	• Water, chemical, and energy use in factories
• Clean by Design by Apparel Impact Institute	• Water, chemical, and energy use in factories

Source: Collected from different websites by the author.

recently to improve the working conditions in various ways. These are also considered as the ways to upgrade the social, economic, and environmental aspects of the factory. The management perception of such initiatives can be evaluated from my experience of a study that seeks to understand the enabling and constraining factors behind the scalability of supply chain initiatives that aim to combine social or environmental benefits with a business case in the garment industry.[4] We studied six initiatives – Better Work, PaCT (Partnership for Cleaner Textile), Clean by Design, Sweden Textile Water Initiative, HER, Benefits for Business and Workers. To understand the challenges of scaling up these projects we conducted interviews of senior management of 43 factories. The research finds that almost all suppliers mentioned the main motivation to introduce these initiatives in their factories was to satisfy a request from their buyers. Retain and please buyers is a crucial factor for the suppliers behind joining these projects. The buyers want to see these projects in the sourcing factories because they are under a lot of pressure from consumers to address social and environmental responsibilities. If the supplier is complying with all of the buyer's checklist, this may help the buyer to retain that supplier. Out of 43, 6 factories did not join these programs because their buyers who were not engaged in these initiatives did not approach them. The other reasons were the company's own goal of sustainability applicable to self-motivated factories, return of investment financially particularly in PaCT.

The IFC's PaCT has two main concerns – first, save the use of water. The country's (Bangladesh) groundwater level has been depleting at an alarming rate, and the most polluted subsector of RMG is the washing-dyeing-finishing unit because it uses the largest amount of water. Second, capacity building. There has been a lot of uncharted territories to be worked on in terms of capacity building, which led the IFC to the conclusion that brand participation is inevitable. In general, the Bangladesh garment factories use almost 300 litres of water to dye one kilogram of fabric, whereas the global standard is around 50–60 litres. From our research, a factory's experience of benefitting from PaCT can explain it better. For instance, one factory was using 120 L of water to dye a kilo of fabric. By involving in the PaCT project water use was brought down to 60 L. It meant the factory was not using groundwater and saved money by not using a water pump. At the same time, due to using less water, the ETP pressure was also reduced. There were also savings from dying. For dyeing, the colours and chemicals needed to be in proportionate amounts to ensure quality. So when the quantity of water was brought down to 60 litres, automatically the quantity of dye was lowered. Previously it required 500 g of dye to colour 1 kg of fabric. That was reduced by 50 g for 60 litres of water. This factory used to dye 40,000 kg of fabric per day before. So if 50 g was reduced, a huge saving was accomplished. Currently this factory dye 80 tonnes of fabric, so in terms of dye and chemicals, the saving is more than a million dollars due to a reduction in water consumption through PaCT.

On the contrary, it was difficult for the HER project to project financial gain for the suppliers because it focusses on health, particularly menstrual hygiene. One of the suppliers shares his experiences of HER health in his factory in the following way.

Box 7.3 Management experience of HER project

The focus of HER project is female hygiene, particularly the menstrual cycle. Many female workers are not aware and don't follow proper hygiene. So, before and after the particular menstrual cycle, their attendance is affected. As most of them don't follow proper hygiene, they become ill, or they can't keep up the pace, thus efficiency deteriorates. That eventually affects our productivity. In this situation, if we implement HER project, that will help to raise awareness, they can learn proper hygiene, and thus stay healthy and increase productivity. HER was proposed by Best Seller, our buyer. But it was implemented by AWAJ foundation. So, when we joined the project, our consent was, according to labour law, we cannot make our workers work for extended hours. So, this activity, peer education, training the peer educators, these have to be done within the working hour. So, that means, if I'm disengaging a certain group of my workers and send them to training that will affect my productivity because we have a chain of production. If we take out five operators from a sewing line, the production is hampered. We can't run that by appointing substitute operators. So, this was a concern for us, if we take out a certain amount of people for 1 hour every week, then "X" amount of production is hampered. We calculated that. And that was the selling point of HER. The initiator of HER project said, the amount of loss you are facing for this project versus the loss you have to carry for the absentee or the extra workers you have to appoint to cover that, that will be compensated. This is very difficult to measure. But, we gave the AWAJ foundation a target, to show us the calculation, and that this will be a win-win project for us. They actually couldn't give that calculation. This was a difficult calculation. There is no concrete way to measure it. No female worker will ever say that they are having their menstrual cycle, that's why they are not comfortable and eventually producing less. So these are very difficult things to assess. I don't think there was a measurable tool. My perspective was a bit different. I could talk to my upper management about it. I told them, let's look at it from a more social return point of view, not an economical one. Think about it: we are training our workers; they are training their neighbours, and this goes on like a chain reaction. So, I'm not keen to find out how much productivity is increasing or the profit is increasing, because we cannot measure it. Rather, I would like to know, what the peer educators are contributing in terms of teaching others. Unfortunately, it never happened. I think it was like, no one was ready to take that level of deep dive and find out. But, I can imagine, if, among our 100 female workers, one can teach a new person outside the factory that was my achievement. So, we were not looking at it from a financial achievement, rather as a social responsibility.

To some suppliers, HER project has a financial outcome. A factory introduced HER because of their concern with menstrual hygiene, maternal health, proper sanitary disposal, and things that would increase the well-being of their female workers. The General Manager of the company reported that earlier where it would take around 75,000 takas to clean the surrounding sewage line; it now costs 10,000 takas. The reason was simple; earlier the female workers used discarded clothes or cheap materials for menstrual hygiene and then just throw it or flush it down the sewerage lines after one time. As the women became more aware, they have started using better hygiene products and not just throwing them away.

For the suppliers, the last motivating factor for joining these supply chain initiatives was reducing audit in the case of Better Work. This initiative focusses on the training of workers on building skills for how to deal with management and to raise issues and assessing compliance to labour laws, educating about core international labour standards, and advising on worker and management dialogue. The ILO's Better Work is designed as an advisory tool to address compliance at workplaces. But the benefit to the suppliers in joining this programme is an audit waiver if that factory is doing business with a buyer partner of Better Work. The buyer is not going to execute its code of conduct or audit inspection rather Better Work report is considered as audit certification.

For the sustainability of upgrading initiatives, a sense of ownership is essential which is missing in the garment supply chain. Above all, an initiative will be truly successful when it takes into account the constructive opinion from both the workers and the owners. It is important to go to the owners before developing a project and ask them what kind of project the initiators of projects should come up with or go to the owners and ask what kind of projects will be beneficial. After collecting this information, an initiator should develop the project in cooperation with the owners. It is essential to develop a project by consulting the suppliers. The programme initiator needs to set up the goal, not the activities, first. It is effective to take the concern of the owners first. And then there is no need for outsiders to push for the project because in that case, the owner will develop the project for their benefit, will try to make the project successful for their benefit. In this way, the project will be more likely to be sustainable.

Source: Research project "Scale Matters: Scalability of business case initiatives in the garment industry" 2018–2020.

7.5 COVID-19 and responsible business

The COVID-19 pandemic has unfolded a dire situation that has forced fashion retailers, brands, and discount stores to shutter stores since large quantities of existing stock in the stores have been unsold. The closed stores of the prime importing countries are a testament to the greatest crisis of the apparel industry in over a generation. Consumers have stayed home to follow social distancing, causing a drastic decrease in demand for new clothes. Factory owners in Bangladesh RMG face financial ruin and most importantly the livelihoods of more than 4 million garment workers are at stake. Nazma Akhtar, a prominent union leader, expressed the vulnerability of the workers in the following way (Suhrawardi, 2020):

> The cruel reality is that the sufferer is our worker, they are the most vulnerable. The manufactures will be losing profit, but it is the worker who will lose their food. We have to think about the people who made you [brands] profit for years. When they need you, you cannot leave them in a starving situation. All these years we worked to make your companies so much profit. We did that together. We should be in this together.

Anner (2020) conducted a survey of the Bangladesh suppliers in March 2020 and revealed the devastating impact of COVID-19 on the suppliers. The research finds 45.8% of suppliers reported cancellation of completed orders by their buyers, 72.1% of buyers refused to pay for raw materials. The study also shows 91.3% of buyers refused to pay the production cost. As a result of the cancellation of orders, 58% of factories surveyed shut down most or all of their operations in Bangladesh. Work orders dropped to 172 in the March–May period, which was 454 in the same period last year, as per the BGMEA data (Ovi, 2020). The garments export of Bangladesh declined by more than 62% in the first 29 days of May 2020 compared with that of the corresponding period last year. The estimation of orders cancelled or put on hold by the buyers ranged from $23 million to $273 million. Table 7.3 shows the status of order and buyers' responses. The BGMEA also proclaims that the factories are now running at only 55% capacity due to lesser work orders (Ovi, 2020). Explaining the devastating impact of the pandemic, Rubana Huq, the president of the BGMEA said (Paton, 2020):

> Our situation is apocalyptic...Brands who were partners last month have all turned into strangers...For them (Western Retailers), it's a question of the survival of the businesses. For us, it's the survival of our 4.1 million workers.

The buyers have used the "force majeure" clause to avoid liability. This clause has released them from their contractual duties due to the COVID-19. Explaining it Alan Behr, a partner at Phillips Nizer, a fashion law firm said, "If you have anything in there (force majeure clause) on disease, pandemics, quarantines, then you have a specific force majeure clause that will probably

Table 7.3 Perception of buyers on the crisis

Buyers	*Order status*	*Comment from buyers*
C&A	Sent a letter to suppliers in March cancelling all orders through to June. Later backtracked, promising to pay for 93% of orders that are finished or in production and negotiate settlements for the remaining 7%. Has started to discuss new orders.	Reaching out to our suppliers to identify ways to mitigate the devastating economic impact of this crisis on suppliers.
Next	Cancelled some orders but will pay for orders that were due to leave supplier factories up to and including April 10. Selecting ranges and continues to order stock for later in the year.	Product teams have cancelled stock that no longer needs an identified stock that can carry over to future seasons. Endeavoured to be fair to suppliers.
Walmart	Will pay for orders, with a few exceptions. Has placed new orders in South and Southeast Asia.	Estimated that such exceptions will amount to less than 2% of the estimated annual private brand apparel orders in Bangladesh.
Gap	Reuters could not determine the status of orders.	Focussed on reducing expenses while doing what is in the best interest of employees, customers, and partners as well as the long-term health of the company. Managing inventory, including identifying those products that can be sold in the short-term, those that can be stored now to be sold later, and those orders that need to be cancelled.
Bestseller	Committed to paying for orders already made and in production, but has negotiated changes in terms with suppliers. Says it is placing a reduced volume of orders for Autumn.	Any changes in terms and volumes have been agreed upon with all suppliers through these individual negotiations and all due invoices to suppliers have been paid to enable suppliers to cover their expenses.
H&M	Will pay for orders and is placing new ones, though the crisis is impacting plans.	Highly value the relationship with suppliers and standby commitments, being transparent and having responsible purchasing practices.
Inditex	Will pay for orders, whether finished or in production.	Ensure that all orders that are in production are completely paid according to the original payment schedule, making full payment even if current circumstances mean that it's not yet possible for the products to be shipped.

(*Continued*)

Buyers	*Order status*	*Comment from buyers*
Marks and Spencer	Paying for orders shipped before March 24, paying for all made garments for almost every order not shipped before March 24.	Have paid for all shipped products and the vast majority of orders will pre-pay for all garments and committed fabric – which is the most expensive cost for a supplier – and across all partners will aim to ensure that no fabric goes to waste and is used at a later date.
Tesco	Committed to paying for orders, shipped or unshipped.	Not changing payment terms or asking for discounts, and will use most of the fabric suppliers have already bought on future orders.
Sainsbury	Has paid for everything manufactured for it.	Have honoured every contract with clothing suppliers.
ASOS	Delayed and cancelled orders worth between 5 million pounds and 6 million pounds ($6 mln to $7.3 mln). Will pay for orders that were shipped by March 13. Negotiating settlements with suppliers individually.	Reviewing stock intake; reducing reliance on categories that have been affected, such as dresses and tailoring; and shifting into higher-demand products, such as loungewear and activewear. As a result, have had to delay some orders and cancel others.
Primark	Will pay for 370 million pounds in orders either finished or in production for handover by April 17. Primark did not say what percentage of its total commitments that represents.	Committed to paying for some 370 million pounds ($450 mln) of additional orders for product over and above the 1.5 billion pounds of stock in stores, in depots, and in transit.
Mango	Will pay for orders already shipped but delaying payment for those in production. Has made new orders from factories in China and Bangladesh.	Have committed to pay for products already shipped and for those that are still in production have negotiated with the suppliers to extend the payment time by one month.
Fast Retailing (Uniqlo)	Has committed to paying for orders and is placing new orders.	Believe that brands have an important role to play in mitigating the humanitarian and economic threats posed by the COVID-19 pandemic.
New Look	Cancelled 20% of spring/summer orders from Bangladesh	Could not place new orders until further notice and would be temporarily postponing outstanding supplier payments until the situation improves.
JC Penney	Delaying payment for orders	Extended payment terms to 60 days.

Source: Dhaka Tribune (May 19, 2020).

be effective for you in negotiations. If it simply says 'act of God,' which nearly all of them say, well you've got a basis for discussion there" (Bain, 2020). As per the "force majeure" if factory owners had already purchased materials, they would need to try to sell them to recoup whatever costs they could. Some retailers, brands, and buyers have agreed to pay for orders that have already been shipped or are in production after a public uproar. Discounts and delayed payment were proposed by few buyers, leaving suppliers struggling to stay inundated.

To understand the impact of the COVID-19 on the suppliers the CED (2020) conducted two surveys. The data of Phase 1 was collected from 1,626 factories in the first week of May, and Phase 2 data was collected from 2,334 factories in mid-June. The objective of these studies is to explore whether the Bangladesh RMG has been able to overcome the disaster. The findings of the Phase 1 survey show 64% of factories were in operation after the pandemic but it increased to 80% in the Phase 2 study. After June, 27.08% of the factories were found to be utilizing more than 80% of their total capacity which was 8% in May 2020. The factories that are currently operational are using 92.1% of their workforce during the pandemic as compared to the pre-pandemic period; it was 57% in Phase 1.

In efforts to face the possible impact of the COVID-19 on the economy, the government of Bangladesh has announced a stimulus package of $590

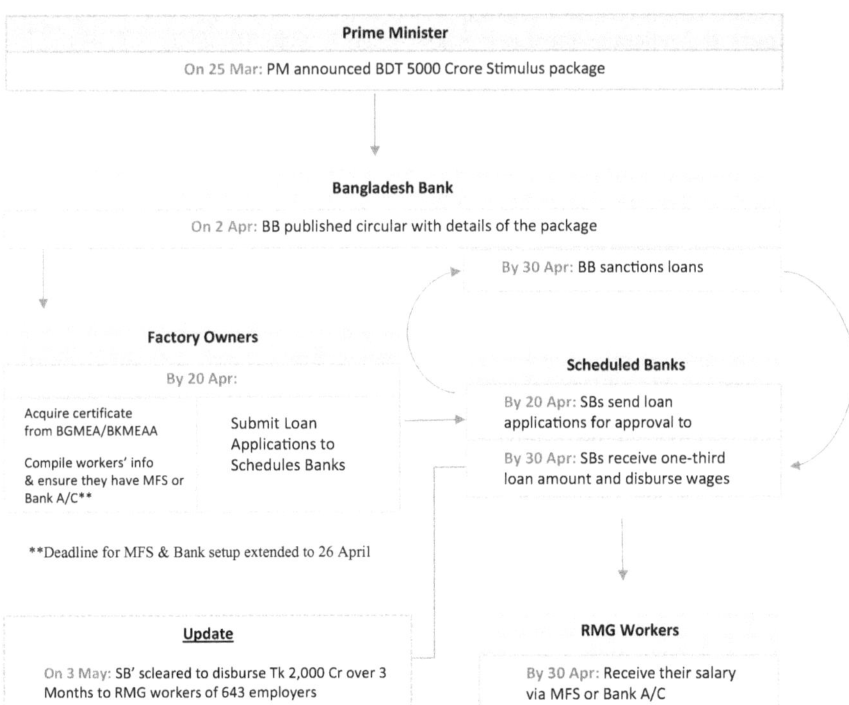

Figure 7.1 Flowchart for stimulus package

million for the RMG industry (Figure 7.1). This fund has been designed as an interest-free loan for the sole purpose of payment of wages and benefits to workers for up to three months (Bangladesh Bank, 2020). However, there has been some criticism of the government's stimulus package by the unions in the BIGD's (2020) study. They raised questions about (a) the adequacy of the fund because the current size of the government's fund is only about 51% of the amount needed to pay the minimum wage for three months and to cover at least 4,000 factories, (b) how much will actually be paid to each worker, and (c) the lack of a needs-based principle in implementing the package (BIGD, 2020). More efforts need to be placed to ensure the transparency of the disbursement of the stimulus package, the accessibility of small factories to be eligible for the funding, the involvement of unions in the process, and a database of workers to monitor and administer the status of the payment.

Notes

1 The management survey was conducted in 2017–2018 as part of a research project. BRAC Institute of Governance and Development (BIGD) at BRAC University in collaboration with the London School of Economics, the University of New South Wales, the Freie University, the University of Gothenburg initiated a research titled, "Changes in the Governance of Garment Global Production Networks: Lead Firm, Supplier and Institutional Responses to the Rana Plaza Disaster." This three-year research project was funded by the Volkswagen Foundation with Wellcome Trust and Riksbanken Jubileumsfond as part of the Europe and Global Challenges Program.

2 The BSCI (Business Social Compliance Initiative) is a social compliance platform that provides a range of practical auditing tools to help its members manage their risk and effectively monitor their supply chain. The ISO refers to a quality management standard used by organizations to prove that they meet up the global labor requirements. It follows a series of regulations to ensure compliance at workplaces. The WRAP (Worldwide Responsible Accredited Production) is an independent, objective, non-profit team of global social compliance experts dedicated to promoting safe, lawful, humane, and ethical manufacturing around the world through certification and education. Sedex is one of the world's leading ethical trade service providers in global supply chains. They provide practical tools, services and a community network to help companies improve their responsible and sustainable business practices, and source responsibly. OEKO-TEX is one of the world's best-known labels for textiles tested for harmful substances. For details see https://www.amfori.org/content/amfori-bsci, https://www.iso.org/home.html, https://wrapcompliance.org/,https://www.sedex.com/, https://www.oeko-tex.com/en/our-standards/standard-100-by-oeko-tex.

3 Management survey 2017–2018.

4 This data was collected in 2018–2019 by the author of this book in a project titled "Scale Matters: Scalability of business case initiatives in the garment industry" funded by Laudes Foundation and conducted in collaboration with Dr Chikako Oka, Prof Niklas Egels-Zandén, and Dr Rachel Alexander. The study seeks to understand the enabling and constraining factors behind the scalability of supply chain initiatives that aim to combine social or environmental benefits with a business case in the garment industry. The final report is available here: https://www.researchgate.net/publication/344150900_SCALE_MATTERS_Scalability_of_Business_Case_Sustainability_Initiatives_in_the_Garment_Industry.

8 Road ahead

The Bangladesh economy grew at 3.5% per year during the first two decades after independence and accelerated to more than 7% in recent years. If Bangladesh can sustain growth at this rate, the income will double every 14 years and will stimulate the development of industries and the service sector. The economy has become resilient to global shocks, and it adjusted well to the global financial crises of 2008. However, while Bangladesh's GDP growth is going up, income inequality has been widening. A study of CPD points out that over the last six years, the income of 5% of the country's wealthy went up by Tk 320 billion and that of 5% of the poorest went down by Tk. 1,058. Despite rising income inequality, Bangladesh is well ahead of both India and Pakistan in almost all human development indicators. The main challenge to the economy now is how to accommodate inclusive growth, a growth process that benefits everyone. It is no doubt Bangladesh holds a key position in Asia as the economy of this South Asian country has been progressively integrating over time, and the probability of its emergence in the foreseeable future is reasonably high. The growth of Bangladesh's economy is now mainly driven by three sectors – agriculture, export-oriented ready-made garment (RMG) industry, and remittance from overseas. Farmers, garment workers and low-skilled overseas workers have transformed the country from a Least Developed to a Lower-Middle-Income country after 49 years of independence.

Out of these three key sectors, the export-oriented garment industry is the engine of the economic growth of Bangladesh as this industry accounts for more than 75% of the export earnings of the country. It is very important to sustain the growth of the second-largest exporter of garments of the world not only for the economy of this emerging Lower-Middle-Income country but also for the social development of Bangladesh. The emphasis is on changing the lives of about 4 million workers. This is the industry through which Bangladeshi women have been able to actively take part in the paid labour market for the first time. However, over the last few years, the participation of women workers in the Ready-Made Garment (RMG) sector's labour force has been on the decline. Rahman's (2018) study on "Revisiting empowerment" introduces the discussion on the rising female unemployment in the

Bangladesh garment sector. The study finds that a 2015 survey by the Asian Centre for Development reported that 65% of workers in the RMG sector were women. In the factories under the ILO RMG programme, it was established that only 58% of the labour force consisted of women, in contrast to the often-repeated statistic that women comprised 80% of the labour force in the garment industries. The executive director of the Bangladesh Institute of Labour Studies also believed that the total number of garment workers in Bangladesh decreased from 4.4 million in 2013 to 3.6 million in 2017. Why is it that this data indicates the declining participation of women in this sector? There is no concrete evidence as to why the participation of female labour in the garment sector is decreasing, and also where they are shifting to and how it has affected their lives. Nonetheless, two propositions can be offered as possible causes of decreasing female engagement in this industry. First, two transnational governance initiatives have emerged from the ashes of the Rana Plaza disaster to ensure factory building safety in Bangladesh since 2013. As per the instructions of the 2013 Accord on Fire and Building Safety and the Alliance for Bangladesh Worker Safety, factories that were located in rented multipurpose buildings were required to be moved to buildings used solely for garment-related production. As a result, most of the garment factories in the capital city, Dhaka, have been in the process of relocation to the periphery or outside the city. It is difficult for the female workers to relocate, as their social life could be hampered as a result of leaving the city. Workers are anxious about their children's future, especially their education – since there is scarcity of quality schools outside the city, and even if there are schools within reach, it is not easy to get admitted. Besides, the husband does not usually leave their current jobs and move to a new place to support their wife. Because of the commitment to family members, female labourers tend to sacrifice their jobs in the garment industry. Second, a positive change has been taking place in the Bangladesh garment industry as new capital investments have been made – a shift from manual labour to automation. The introduction of more advanced technology is the current demand of the global supply chain, and as such, large garment companies in Bangladesh have adapted to this change for the sake of quality garments and mass production. Technology is in the process of replacing labour; dependency on automation has resulted in the reduction of the size of the workforce. This could also explain why many workers, perhaps disproportionately women, were removed from the workforce.

As a result of the two propositions mentioned above, the number of female labourers in the garment sector is being steadily reduced, but the question remains – what other options are available to them? Because of the huge illiteracy rate, these workers are not able to turn to other sectors. These female workers have already had the experience of emancipation from traditional household patriarchy, so most of them would presumably be reluctant to work as housemaids. A significant number of women work in the construction sector, but this is an occupation that is considered beneath that of the garment workers in the occupational hierarchy. Finding work abroad as a migrant labourer could be an option, but it depends on how desperate they are to find work outside the country, leaving their family behind in the process. Altogether, what is alarming is that there is no visible alternative opportunity insight. Does it mean that these once-empowered women garment workers, after losing their jobs, are slowly returning to the life they had before joining the garment industry? That in this process they are losing their status of empowerment and left with very little choice? Indeed, it would be unfortunate to witness a step back from the progress that Bangladesh as a country has made in the last few decades, especially in the garment sector. As such, the visibility and lack of participation of women in the sector raise some serious questions which policymakers must promptly address and take into consideration.

For the sustainable growth of the Bangladesh RMG, along with revisiting women empowerment, the future of small factories is at stake since the Rana Plaza tragedy. About 2,200 RMG factories were governed by the Accord and Alliance (AA), and 1,549 fell under the government's DIFE. The factories under AA fulfilled the requirements of these initiatives for the sake of getting the order from global buyers and retailers. Only the complete remediation prescribed by the inspection team of the AA ensured the approval of both approaches. However, the majority of small factories under AA as well as DIFE struggled to arrange the funds to invest in the remediation of their factories. The failure to do this has resulted in the closing of a minimum of 800 factories. It's very difficult for small factories to comply with the global labour standard because a compliant workplace requires investment which they don't have. This unaffordability initiates an opportunity for their buyers to squeeze them leaving no bargaining power and ending up with a less competitive price of their products. As is evident in Chapter 4, dealing with these challenges leads to becoming a subcontractor, unhealthy workplaces, and finally business unsustainability. Forecasting the future of small factories one of the owners said:

> Small factories will be out of business as they are mostly inefficient and non-compliant. Here the intervention of the government is very important. It takes time to produce an entrepreneur class. If we lose small garment owners it's not good for the country's economy. Rather we should get in touch with their financial problems, arrange low-interest bank loans, and also expect support from other stakeholders so that they remain in this industry.

This is exactly what is required. The policymakers seem to be concerned more with the cream factories leaving behind the small factories from their action plan, and since small factories are far away from the interests of policymakers the management of these small factories can't do more.

Despite the bleak future of small factories, the large garment firms are in the process of expansion and to some extent, medium factories are also following the same direction. These export-oriented RMG companies have the vision to have a greater impact on the industry. With a skilled workforce, their continuous effort is to increase the annual turnover and being reputed locally and globally depending on its diverse set of sustainability activities and collaborating with international development partners. The second generation of young entrepreneurs, often educated abroad, has been growing and pushing industrialization forward. A gradual transformation of the industry is taking place where a taste of professionalism and corporate model is visible. The case studies of a medium and a large factory in Chapter 5 show that significant changes have been brought in management to improve professionalism by offering various training. In addition to social compliance, welfare programmes have been offered to motivate workers and reduce labour migration. There has also been an effort to improve their relationship with buyers, although they are disappointed with the endless decline of the price of their products. In spite of this, management endeavours towards long-term buyer relation because it ensures business sustainability as well as healthy business. And continuous growth of order expands the continuous growth of the factory and its production process. The most important thing is that buyers have a corporate sustainability strategy that covers the quality improvement of their business and focusses on social and environmental sustainability. A long-term relationship not only ensures orders from buyers but allows the factory to take different actions for the betterment of the working environment.

Since most buyers have offices in Bangladesh, management attends the meetings, trainings, and seminars organized by these buyers. Their presence in the sourcing country generates an opportunity to be closely involved in different capacity-building projects, as is evident in Chapter 7. In order to scale up the supply chain initiatives, the suppliers need to have confidence in the outcome of these projects, and the buyers need to prevent the sending of a wrong signal. According to a member of senior management:

> We are scared. Why? Suppose, a buyer has offered us a program for sustainability. Then researchers have assessed the performance and found that our production has increased by 10 per cent after adopting the program. Immediately we became pleased. But then in the next meeting the brand told me that our productivity has increased, so we should provide them a revised lower price. So how would we consider sustainability?

For the sake of sustainability and scaling up of initiatives, Oka et al.'s (2020) research project recommend that the buyers should systematically reward more sustainable suppliers and the initiators need to target beyond "cream" factories and cater to factories that are more likely to benefit from interventions. In addition, the suppliers should be open to considering business cases presented by initiatives and seek help in measuring impact and should ask brands to publicly recognize engagement in sustainability efforts. For the donors of initiatives, the effort should be to reduce overlap and duplication, prioritize initiatives that are coordinating or consolidating with other initiatives. It is also essential to promote collaboration among members as well as between initiatives to achieve greater impact and efficiency. Above all, an initiative will be truly successful when it takes into account the constructive opinion from both the workers and the owners. Before developing a project, the project initiator should ask the garment owners what kind of project will be beneficial for the company. A project should be developed by consulting the factory management. The project team should not set up their goals and set the activities at first place. One needs to form the project with the owners and then there is no need for outsiders to push for the project because, in that case, the owner will develop the project for their own benefit and will try to make it successful.

The buyer-supplier relationship still needs to be improved, as is evident from the analysis of the impact of AA on the Bangladesh RMG in Chapter 6. These two transnational initiatives have had a positive effect on factories in terms of structural, fire, and electric safety. The management has been able to understand how to maintain the safety of their factory buildings by working closely with AA. At the same time, they have faced some challenges in the process of remediation and the limited support from buyers, particularly the unavailability of financial assistance from buyers has made it difficult for the suppliers to implement the CAPs. Finding no alternative, the management has paid the cost of remediation from its sources. Since the approval of AA has become the determinant factor of getting orders from buyers, these two initiatives have created an opportunity for the buyers to extend their asymmetric power relationships with suppliers. At present, the RMG Sustainability Council, introduced by the BGMEA, has replaced the AA and is set to work in cooperation with the government of Bangladesh and global stakeholders. Further research is required to find out the capacity of the Bangladesh government and local stakeholders to continue the works started by the transnational agencies. The main challenge, as argued by Anner (2018), is to build up the capacity of the state to take over. The New York University (NYU) Stern report on Rana Plaza prepared by Barrett et al. (2018) has also questioned the state's capacity. One way to do this would be a comprehensive analysis of the initiatives taken by different stakeholders to explore which programmes have been effective. In this context, the recommendation of Barrett et al. (2018: 26) of the NYU Stern Business School is relevant:

> ...the Bangladeshi government should convene a shared responsibility task force comprised of local factory owners and industry trade associations, Western brand and retailers, European and North American governments, civil society organizations and unions, the World Bank and its affiliate the IFC, and philanthropic organizations.

According to Barrett et al. (2018), the government, in collaboration with other local and global stakeholders, would lead the daunting challenge of finding out how many factories have not completed CAPs under the Accord, Alliance, and National Initiative, and how many require inspection outside of these three bodies. Then the total cost of remediation would be calculated and funds would be raised from different stakeholders – government, owners' associations, brands and retailers, development partners, national and international financial institutions, NGOs, unions, and international philanthropy. After a thorough and rigorous assessment, the resulting remediation fund would be administered by the government to ensure a transparent and accountable monitoring and maintenance system. By working in this way, a culture of safety needs to be institutionalized not only in the garment industry but also gradually in other sectors by learning lessons from the apparel experiences. This includes not only lessons regarding safety but also those regarding the importance of shared responsibility.

Addressing a skilled workforce is another concern. The Bangladesh RMG industry started its journey in 1978 and 41 years later, we are still heavily dependent on imported skills at the management level. The whole education sector has failed for not taking this problem seriously. It seems foreigners are keener to study our garments sector than us. In one of my research projects, students of Kennesaw State University in the U.S. do Skype classes with my students to understand the Bangladesh garment industry. They have designed the course in light of our garments industry, but we don't offer any courses on our own garments industry in most of the universities. Our educational institutions are not creating enough skilled management level people for the RMG sector. Out of 126 universities (46 public and 80 private), there are two universities in the country – BGMEA University of Fashion and Technology (BUFT) and Bangladesh University of Textiles (BUTEX) – that have been established for the garments and textiles industry specifically. Among private universities, BUFT is ranked 25th and BUTEX 9th among public universities. Although they are not the leading universities in the country, so far, they have been doing a commendable job of producing graduates who have the skills necessary for the industry. For example, Ms Shwapna Bhowmick graduated from BUFT and is now the Country Manager of Marks & Spencer in Bangladesh. But obviously, it is insufficient considering the volume and growth of the industry in the country. In other universities, there are some degrees, such as textile and industrial engineering, that also fulfil the demands of the sector. Although there are 80 private universities in the county, only a handful of them offer industrial engineering. Most universities do not offer courses like industrial relations, labour management, occupational health, and safety. Even leading private universities do not have a centre on Corporate Social Responsibility. The grooming of students to become smart merchandisers who can negotiate with buyers is also missing in our curriculum. Courses should be designed in a way that connects classrooms with industries. To ensure the structural safety of factory buildings, we have an adequate number of civil engineers, but the contribution of private universities in this field is minimal. The era of complacency is over, RMG is about to face challenges from automation and competition, and the industry is not ready to produce a skilled workforce.

Despite this drawback, according to the Mckinsey Report 2019, Bangladesh is still seen as the most attractive destination country for buyers, but the gap it has with Vietnam is closing (Berg et al., 2019). Bangladesh, still, is the second-largest exporter of garments in the global market but its future has recently been threatened by the pandemic. More than 300 factories were initially closed because of COVID-19. A positive lesson to be taken from the COVID-19 as argued by Mostafiz Uddin is greater collaboration among garment manufacturers globally. The solidarity of suppliers is required not only from the local context but also from the global landscape since all suppliers have faced a global and common problem. Criticizing the "divide and rule" approach of the MNCs, Mostafiz Uddin (The Daily Star, 2020) has raised some questions to think about for the global suppliers:

> As garment manufacturers, can we not - collectively - call on brands to avoid the questionable usage of the "force majeure" legal remedy which is seeing brands walk away from contracts without any financial repercussions while leaving the supplier financially liable? Can we not agree at a global level that the kind of behavior we have seen from some brands - such as canceling ready orders then ignoring all contact from beleaguered suppliers - will simply not be accepted?

During the pandemic, it seems there is a difficult choice for the government – saving lives or the economy. Bangladesh is considered a role model for other developing economies in achieving sustainable development goals. Bangladesh has been the fastest-growing economy in the Asia-Pacific region, and lately, it's been closing in on double-digit annual growth in its GDP. This achievement has been under threat due to the impact of the pandemic on the economy. In 2019, 20% of people were below the poverty line, but as of the pandemic, it has increased to 30%, i.e., 50 million people (Rahman, 2020). The global strategy of lockdown, as argued by the policymakers, seems to be ineffective in a country like Bangladesh, where the informal economy contributes to more than 80% of the country's growth and the garment sector is the dominant export earning sector. The government has provided a stimulus package for the RMG in efforts to face the possible impact of COVID-19 on the economy. The garment entrepreneurs can avail of this government fund as a loan to pay wages and allowances to the workers and other employees. But the question is how long can the government provide such a safety net? Is Bangladesh's RMG on its way to recovery from the COVID-19 that put the livelihoods of 4 million workers endangered? We believe that if we stay afloat, the business will follow – those days are gone. It is time to address the sustainability issues in earnest. "Business-as-usual" won't take the industry much further from here.

Bibliography

Absar, S. S. (2001). "Women's voice: Conditions, concerns and need of garment workers in Bangladesh." In P. Paul-Majumder and B. Sen (Eds.), *Growth of garment industry in Bangladesh: Economic and social dimension* (pp. 132–140). Dhaka: BIDS.

Afsar, R. (2001). "Female labour migration and urban adaptation." In P. Paul-Majumder and B. Sen (Eds.), *Growth of garment industry in Bangladesh: Economic and social dimension* (pp. 106–131). Dhaka: BIDS.

Afsar, R. (2002). "Gender dimensions of labour migration in Dhaka city's formal manufacturing sector." In C. Miller and J. Vivian (Eds.), *Women's employment in the textile manufacturing sectors of Bangladesh and Morocco* (pp. 103–149). Geneva: UNDP.

Ahmad, N. (1976). *A new economic geography of Bangladesh.* New Delhi: Vikas Publication House.

Akram, T. (2005). "Ineffective privatisation of public enterprises: The case of Bangladesh." In R. Sobhan (Ed.), *Privatisation in Bangladesh: An agenda in search of a policy* (pp. 105–156). Dhaka: The University Press Limited.

Alliance. (2016). Strategy. http://www.bangladeshworkersafety.org/progress-impact/strategy

Anner, M. (2012). "Corporate social responsibility and freedom of association rights." *Politics and Society* 40(4), 609–644.

Anner, M. (2018). "Binding power: The sourcing squeeze, workers' rights, and building safety in Bangladesh since Rana Plaza." CGWR Research Report, Pennsylvania State University. http://lser.la.psu.edu/gwr/documents/CGWR2017ResearchReportBindingPower.pdf (accessed 3 February 2019).

Anner, M. (2020). "Abandoned? The impact of Covid-19 on workers and businesses at the bottom of global garment supply chains." n.p.: Research report, March 27, 2020. Centre for Global Workers.' Right, Pennsylvania State University.

Anner, M., J. Blair and J. Blasy. (2013). "Toward joint liberty on global supply chains: Addressing the root causes of labor violations in international subcontracting networks." *Company Labor Law and Political Journal* 35(1), 1–43.

Anton, T. and P. Osterman. (1994). *The mutual gains enterprise: Forging a winning partnership among labor, management and government.* Boston, MA: Harvard Business School Press.

Appelbaum, R. P. (2004). "Assessing the impact of the phasing-out of the agreement on textile and clothing on apparel exports on the least developed and developing countries." A report conducted in part for the United Nations conference on trade and development, and in part for Sweatshop Watch. Santa Barbara, Center for Global Studies, University of California.

Asian Development Bank (ADB). (2001). *Women in Bangladesh*. Manila: ADB.

Bain, M. (2020) "More than a million garment workers are out of work because of coronavirus." *Quartz*. April 1, 2020. https://qz.com/1828541/covid-19-leads-to-one-million-garment-workers-unemployed.

Bair, J., M. Anner and J. Blasi. (2017). "Sweatshops and the search for solutions, yesterday and today." In R. Prentice and G. De Neve (Eds.), *Unmaking the global sweatshop: Health and safety of the world's garment workers* (pp. 29–56). Philadelphia: University of Pennsylvania Press.

Bair, J., M. Anner and J. Blasi. (2020). "The political economy of private and public regulation in post-Rana Plaza Bangladesh." *Industrial & Labor Relations Review* XX(X), 1–26. doi: 10.1177/0019793920925424.

Bangladesh Bank. (2019). Remittance data. https://www.bb.org.bd/econdata/wageremitance.php.

Bangladesh Bureau of Statistics (BBS). (1994). *Bangladesh data sheet*. Dhaka: Bangladesh Bureau of Statistics (BBS).

Bangladesh Bureau of Statistics (BBS). (2015). *Statistical year book*. Dhaka: Bangladesh Bureau of Statistics (BBS).

Baran, P. (1957). *The political economy of growth*. New York: Monthly Review Press.

Barrett, P. M., D. Baumann-Pauly and A. Gu. (2018). *Five years after Rana Plaza: The way forward*. New York: NYU Stern, Center for Business and Human Rights.

Barrientos, S., G. Gereffi and A. Rossi. (2010). "Economic and social upgrading in global production networks: Developing a framework for analysis." *International Labor Review* 150(3–4), 319–340.

Berg, A., S. Hedrich, P. Ibanez, S. Kappelmark, K. Magnus and M. Seeger. (2019). Fashion's new must have: Sustainable sourcing at scale. McKinsey Apparel CPO Survey Report, October, 2019. https://www.mckinsey.com/industries/retail/our-insights/fashions-new-must-have-sustainable-sourcing-at-scale.

Bernhardt, T. and W. Milberg. (2011). "Economic and social upgrading in global value chains: Analysis of horticulture, apparel, tourism and mobile telephones." Working paper 2011/06. Department of Economics of the New School for Social Research, New York. http://www.capturingthegains.org/pdf/ctg-wp-2011-6.pdf.

Bertocci, P. J. (1977). "Review of Bangladesh: The test case for development by Just Faaland, J. R. Parkinson." *Journal of Asian Studies* 36(4), 783–784.

BGMEA. (2016). Notice. http://www.bgmea.com.bd/home/media/Notice.

BGMEA. (2020). Trade information. http://www.bgmea.com.bd/home/pages/tradeinformation.

Bhattacharya, D. and M. Rahman. (2001). "Bangladesh's apparel sector: Growth trends and the Post-MFA challenges." In P. Paul-Majumder and B. Sen (Eds.), *Growth of garment industry in Bangladesh: Economic and social dimension* (pp. 2–26). Dhaka: BIDS.

BIGD. (2020). "Taka 5000 crore novel corona financial stimulus package for export-oriented industries: RMG trade union responses." Research report Gender series 6, Rapid research response to COVID-19, BRAC Institute of Governance and Development (BIGD), BRAC University. June 18, 2020.

BKMEA. (2016). Note for Buyer (Choose Bangladesh, Source from Bangladesh!). http://www.bkmea.com/note_for_buyer.

Black, Z. (2020) "Bullying' clothing companies are asking struggling suppliers for discounts." *The Daily Star.* https://thenewdaily.com.au/finance/consum/kmart-mosaic-coroner/2020/05/13avirus.

Bloom, N., E. Brynjolfsson, L. Foster, R. Jarmin, M. Patnaik, I. S. Eksten and J. V. Reenen. (2017). *Adding a piece to the productivity puzzle: Management practices.* https://voxeu.org/article/management-practices-and-productivity.

Board of Investment (BoI). (2002). *Bangladesh—Economy and business, trade and investment.* http://www.boi.gov.bd/ (accessed 30 July 2003).

Catholic Agency for Overseas Development (CAFOD). (1998). *The Asian garment industry and globalisation.* http://www.cafod.org.uk/policy/garment_industry.shtml (accessed 15 June 2003).

CED. (2020). Rapid survey. Centre for entrepreneurship and development, BRAC University. http://ced.bracu.ac.bd/mib-rapid-survey/.

Chen, M. (1995). "A matter of survival: Women's right to employment in India and Bangladesh." In M. C. Nussbaum and J. Glover (Eds.), *Women, culture, and development: A study of human capabilities* (pp. 37–57). Oxford/New York: Clarendon Press/Oxford University Press.

Choi, Y. P., H. S. Chung and N. Marian. (1985). *The multi-fibre arrangement in theory and practice.* London/Dover, NH: Frances Pinter.

Clean Clothes Campaign. (2010). At least 28 more garment workers die in Bangladeshi factory fire. 14 October 2010 issue. http://www.cleanclothes.org/news/2010/12/14/at-least-28-more-garment-workers-die-in-bangladeshi-factory-fire.

CPD. (2018). Ongoing upgradation in RMG enterprises: preliminary results from a survey. Conference presentation, Centre for Policy Dialogue 3 March, 2018, Dhaka. https://www.researchgate.net/publication/325567646_Ongoing_Upgradation_in_RMG_Enterprises_Preliminary_Results_from_a_Survey.

CPD. (2019). *New dynamics in Bangladesh's apparels enterprises: Perspectives on upgradation, restructuring and compliance assurance.* Project Report, May 20, 2019. Dhaka: Centre for Policy Dialogue.

Custers, P. (1997). *Capital accumulation and women's labour in Asian economies.* London: Zed.

Cyber Bangladesh. (2002). Bangladesh Human Rights practices 1994. http://www.cyberbangladesh.org/sec6.html (accessed 16 June 2003).

Dhaka Tribune. (2020). Covid-19: Fashion brands cut orders from Bangladesh, Asian garments. May 19, 2020. Dhaka Tribune. https://www.dhakatribune.com/world/2020/05/19/fashion-brands-cut-orders-from-bangladesh-asian-garments.

Dicken, P. (1998). *Global shift: Transforming the world economy.* London: Paul Chapman Publishing Ltd.

Dijkstra, A. G. (2002). "The effectiveness of policy conditionality: Eight country experiences." *Development and Change* 33(2), 307–334.

Donaghey, J. and J. Reinecke. (2017). "When industrial democracy meets corporate social responsibility—A comparison of the Bangladesh accord and alliance as responses to the Rana Plaza disaster." *British Journal of Industrial Relations* 56(1), 14–42.

Donaghey, J. and J. Reinecke. (2018). "When industrial democracy meets corporate social responsibility—A comparison of the Bangladesh Accord and Alliance as responses to the Rana Plaza Disaster." *British Journal of Industrial Relations* 56(1), 14–42.

Dutt, K., R. Dasgupta and A. Chatterjee. (1973). *Bangladesh economy: An analytical study*. New Delhi: People's Publication House.

Edwards, R. (1979). *Contested terrain: The transformation of the workplace in the twentieth century*. New York: Basic Books.

Ellis-Petersen, H. and R. Ahmed. "Bangladesh garment factories reopen despite coronavirus threat to workers." *The Guardian*. https://www.theguardian.com/global-development/2020/may/11/bangladesh-garment-factories-reopen-despite-coronavirus-threat-to-workers.

EPB. (2006). *Export statistics by export promotion bureau*. http://www.epb.gov.bd/ (accessed 10 August 2006).

Esbenshade, J. L. (2004). *Monitoring sweatshops: Workers, consumers and the global apparel industry*. Philadelphia, PA: Temple University Press.

European Commission. (2015). *Bangladesh sustainability compact: Technical status report*. http://trade.ec.europa.eu/doclib/docs/2015/april/tradoc_153390.pdf.

Export Promotion Bureau (EPB). (2006). *Export statistics*. http://www.epb.gov.bd/ (accessed 10 August 2006).

Faaland, J. and J. R. Parkinson. (1976). *Bangladesh: The test case of development*. London: C. Hurst.

Financial Express. (2019). *RMG hourly productivity still lower in BD*. 6 May. https://today.thefinancialexpress.com.bd/last-page/rmg-hourly-productivity-still-lower-in-bd-1557082051.

Frank, A. G. (1966). *The development of underdevelopment*. New York: Monthly Review Press.

Fukunishi, T. (2014). *The Bangladeshi garment sector in the liberalised market: Is upgrading needed*. Japan: Institute of Developing Economies, Japan External Trade Organization.

Gerard, C., J. B. Donges, J. Waelbroeck, J. de la Torre, M. I. Alasdair and M. Wolf. (1981). *MFA forever? Future of the arrangement for trade in textiles*. London: Trade Policy Research Centre.

Gereffi, G. and J. Lee. (2016). "Economic and social upgrading in global value chains and industrial clusters: Why governance matters." *Journal of Business Ethics* 133(1), 25–38.

Haque, M. S. (2002). "Globalization, new political economy, and governance: A Third World viewpoint." *Administrative Theory and Praxis* 24(1), 103–124.

Harris, N., L. Bulbul, K. Mainuddin, X. Meng, S. Naguib and S. Srinivas. (1999). "Garment-making and urbanisation: An introductory study of four cases." Working Paper Series 6. Washington, DC: The World Bank.

Hensler, B. and J. Blasi. (2013). "Making Global Corporations' Labor Rights Commitments Legally Enforceable: The Bangladesh Breakthrough." Workers Right Consortium. April 21, 2018.

Hewett, P. and S. Amin. (2000). "Assessing the impact of garment work on quality of life measures." In P. Paul-Majumder and B. Sen (Eds.), *Growth of garment industry in Bangladesh: Economic and social dimension* (pp. 145–171). Dhaka: BIDS.

Hodson, R. (1999). "Organizational anomie and worker consent." *Work and Occupations* 26, 292–323.

Humphrey, C. E. (1990). *Privatization in Bangladesh: Economic transition in a poor country*. Boulder, CO: Westview Press.

Huq, F. A., A. N. Chowdhury and R. D. Klassenb. (2016). "Social management capabilities of multinational buying firms and their emerging market suppliers: An exploratory study of the clothing industry." *Journal of Operations Management* 46: 19–37.

Ichniowski, C., T. A. Kochan, D. Levine, C. Olson and G. Strauss. (1996). "What works at work: Overview and assessment." *Industrial Relations* 35(3), 299–331.

International Trade Statistics Yearbook. (2017). https://comtrade.un.org/.

Islam, A. M. and M. Quddus. (1996). "The export garment industry in Bangladesh: A potential catalyst for breakthrough." In N. M. Wahid and C. E. Weis (Eds.), *The economy of Bangladesh: Problems and prospects* (pp. 167–198). Westport, CT/ London: Praeger Publishers.

Islam, M., R. Khan and C. Wichterich. (2015). "Safety and labour conditions: The accord and the national tripartite plan of action for the garment industry in Bangladesh." Global Labour University Working Paper, p. 38.

Kabeer, N., M. Solaiman and L. Huq. (2020) "Paradigm shift or business as usual?" Workers' views on multi-stakeholder initiatives in Bangladesh. n.p.: Development and Change. pp. 1–39.

Kabeer, N. and S. Mahmud. (2004). "Globalization, gender and poverty: Bangladesh women workers in export and local markets." *Journal of International Development* 16(1), 93–109.

Karim, A. (1996). "An analysis of privatisation initiative in Bangladesh." In A. N. M. Wahid and C. E. Weis (Eds.), *The economy of Bangladesh: Problems and prospects* (pp. 1–16). Westport, CT/London: Praeger Publishers.

Khan, S. (1988). *The fifty percent: Women in development and policy in Bangladesh.* Dhaka: The University Press Ltd.

Kibria, N. (1995). "Culture, social class and income control in the lives of women garment workers in Bangladesh." *Gender and Society* 9(3), 289–309.

Kibria, N. (2002). "Becoming a garment worker: The mobilization of women into the garment factories of Bangladesh." In C. Miller and J. Vivian (Eds.), *Women's employment in the textile manufacturing sectors of Bangladesh and Morocco* (pp. 151–177). Geneva: UNDP.

Kochan, T. A. and P. Osterman. (1994). *The mutual gains enterprise: Forging a winning partnership among labor, management and government.* Boston, MA: Harvard Business School Press.

Labowitz, S. and D. Baumann-Pauly. (2014). *Business as usual is not an option: Supply chains and sourcing after Rana Plaza.* New York: Center for Business and Human Rights.

Lincoln, J. and A. Kalleberg. (1990). *Culture, control, and commitment: A study of work organization and work attitudes in the United States and Japan.* Cambridge: Cambridge University Press.

Living Wage Benchmark Report. (2015–2016). https://www.isealalliance.org/sites.

Locke, R., M. Amengual and A. Mangla. (2009). "Virtue out of necessity? Compliance, commitment, and the improvement of labor conditions in global supply chains." *Politics & Society* 37(3), 319–351. http://doi.org/10.1177/0032329209338922

Locke, R. M. (2013). *The promise and limits of private power: Promoting labor standards in a global economy.* New York: Cambridge University Press.

Locke, R. M., F. Qin and A. Brause. (2006). "Does monitoring improve labor standards? Lessons from Nike." MIT Sloan Research paper No. 4612-06.

Locke, R. M. and M. Romis. (2006). "Beyond corporate codes of conduct: Work organization and labor standards in two Mexican garment factories." MIT Sloan Research paper No. 4617-06.

Macchiavello, R., A. Rabbani and C. Woodruff. (2015). "The market for training services: a demand experiment with Bangladeshi garment factories." *American Economic Review* 105(5), 300–304.

Mahmood, S. A. (2002). "How the Bangladesh garment Industry took off in the early eighties: The role of policy reforms and diffusion of good practices." *Alochona Magazine*. October 2002.

Mallon, R. D. and J. J. Stern. (1991). "The political economy of trade and industrial policy reform in Bangladesh." In D. H. Perkins and M. Roemer (Eds.), *Reforming economic systems in developing countries*. Cambridge, MA: Harvard Institute for International Development.

Management Survey. (2017–2018). Garment supply chain governance project. Freie University, Berlin. Project website: https://www.wiwiss.fu-berlin.de/forschung/Garments/index.html.

Merk, J. (2011). "Production beyond the horizon of consumption: Spatial fixes and anti-sweatshop struggles in the global athletic footwear industry." *Global Society* 25(1), 73–95.

Milberg, W. and D. Winkler. (2011). "Economic and social upgrading in global production networks: Problems of theory and measurement." *International Labour Review* 150(3–4), 341–365.

Mirza, M. (2019). "State-business nexus in Bangladesh: Quick rental power plants in perspective." In M. Tanzimuddin Khan and M. Sajjadur Rahman (Eds.), *Neoliberal development in Bangladesh*. Dhaka: The University Press Limited, pp. 113–136.

Misra, M. (2019). "Interrogating the "peasant question" in post-reform Bangladesh." In M. Tanzimuddin Khan and M. Sajjadur Rahman (Eds.), *Neoliberal Development in Bangladesh*. Dhaka: The University Press Limited, pp. 65–88.

Mueller, C. W., S. D. Coster and S. B. Estes. (2001). "Sexual harassment in the workplace: Unanticipated consequences of modern social control in organizations." *Work and Occupations* 28(4), 411–446.

Mujeri, M. and B. Khondker. (2002). *Poverty implications of trade liberalization in Bangladesh: A general equilibrium approach*. http://sed-trade-forum.itcilo.org/eng/Papers/Other/MustafaPov.pdf (accessed 24 January 2006).

Nathan, D. and S. Sarkar. (2011). "Blood on your mobile phone? Capturing the gains for artisanal miners, poor workers and women." Capturing the Gains for Artisanal Miners, Poor Workers and Women (February 23, 2011).

Neve, G. D. and R. Prentice. (2017). *Unmaking the global sweatshop: Health and safety of the world's garment workers*. Philadelphia: University of Pennsylvania Press.

New Age. (2020). The curse of default loans. March 14, 2020. https://www.newagebd.net/article/102206/the-curse-of-default-loans.

New York Times. (2013). *Garment trade wields power in Bangladesh. July 25, 2013.* https://www.nytimes.com/2013/07/25/world/asia/garment-trade-wields-power-in-bangladesh.html.

Oka, C., N. Egels-Zanden, S. Rahman and R. Alexander. (2020). Scale matters: Scalability of business case sustainability initiatives in the garment industry. Project report, September 2020, Royal Holloway, University of London.

O'Rourke, D. (1997). *Smoke from a hired gun*. San Francisco, CA: Transnational Resource and Action Center.

Ovi, I. H. *Apparel exporters see 62% drop in new orders*. Dhaka Tribune. June 15, 2020. https://www.dhakatribune.com/business/economy/2020/06/15/apparel-exporters-see-62-drop-in-new-orders.

Palmer, G. F. (1994). *The EIU global privatisation model: A practical guide to the process and practitioners.* London: The Economist Intelligence Unit.

Pahle, S. (2010). "The rise and demise of the 'Social Clause' proposal in the 1990s: Implications of a discourse theoretical reading." *Labor History* 51(3), 389–410.

Paton, E. "Our Situation is Apocalyptic': Bangladesh Garment Workers Face Ruin." *The New York Times.* March 3, 2020. https://www.nytimes.com/2020/03/31/fashion/coronavirus-bangladesh.html.

Paul-Majumder, P. and A. Begum. (2000). "The gender imbalances in the export oriented garment industry in Bangladesh." Policy research report on gender and development. Working paper series No. 12. Washington: Gendernet, World Bank.

Paul-Majumder, P. and S. C. Zohir. (1994). "Dynamics of wage employment: A case of employment in the garment industry." *Bangladesh Development Studies* 22 (2–3), 179–216.

Pruett, D., J. Merk and N. Ascoly. (2005). *Looking for a quick fix: How weak social auditing is keeping workers in sweatshops.* Amsterdam: Clean Clothes Campaign.

PwC Bangladesh. (2018). *Fuelling business growth through values and purpose in a digital age. PwC Bangladesh Family Business Survey 2018.* https://www.pwc.in/assets/pdfs/research-insights/2019/pwc-bangladesh-family-business-survey.pdf.

Quadir, F. (2000). "The political economy of pro-market reforms in Bangladesh: regime consolidation through economic liberalization?" *Contemporary South Asia* 9(2), 197–212.

Quddus, M. and S. Rashid. (2000). *Entrepreneurs and economic development: The remarkable story of garment exports from Bangladesh.* Dhaka: The University Press Limited.

Rahman, S. and K. M. Rahman. (2020). "Multi-actor initiatives after Rana Plaza: Factory Mangers' views." *Development and Change* 51(5), 1331–1359.

Rahman, M. and Z. Bakht. (1997). "Constraints to industrial development: Recent reforms and future directions." In M. G. Qibria (Ed.), *The Bangladesh economy in transition.* Delhi/New York: Oxford University Press, pp. 77–114.

Rahman, S. (2009). "Socio-economic vulnerability and neo-liberalism: Lessons from Bangladesh." *South Asia Research* 29(3), 235–254.

Rahman, S. (2014). *Broken promises of globalization: The case of the Bangladesh garment industry.* Lanham, MD: Lexington Books.

Rahman, S. (2018). "Revisiting empowerment: Rising female employment in the Bangladesh garment sector." *Journal of Human Geography* 11(2), 35–37.

Rahman, S. (2019). "Neo-liberalism, state and labor: Reflections on the garment industry." In M. Tanzimuddin Khan and M. Sajjadur Rahman (Ed.), *Neoliberal development in Bangladesh.* Dhaka: The University Press Limited, pp. 89–112.

Rahman, S. (2019). "Post-Rana Plaza responses: Changing role of the Bangladesh government." In S. Saxena (Ed.), *Labour, global supply chains and the garment industry in South Asia.* London and New York: Routledge, pp. 123–140.

Rahman, S. (2020). What the pandemic means for RMG. Dhaka Tribune, May 5, 2020. https://www.dhakatribune.com/opinion/op-ed/2020/05/05/what-the-pandemic-means-for-rmg.

Reinecke, J., J. Donaghey, N. Bocken and L. Lauriano. (2019). *Business models and labor standards: Making the connection.* London: Ethical Trading Initiative.

Representation of the People Act. (2013). *Amendment 2013.* http://www.parliament.gov.bd/index.php/en/acts-of-19th-session/1909-representation-of-the-people-amendment-act-2013.

Rizvi, N. (1983). "Life cycle, food behaviour and nutrition of women in Bangladesh." In J. Huq, H. Begum, K. Salahuddin and S. R. Qadir (Eds.), *Women in Bangladesh: Some socio-economic issues* (pp. 70–79). Dhaka: Women for Women.

Rock, M. (2001). "The rise of Bangladesh Independent Garment-Workers' Union (BIGU)." In H. Jane and B. Andrew (Eds.), *Organising labour in globalising Asia* (pp. 27–47). London/New York: Routledge.

Rodríguez-Garavito, C. A. (2005). "Global governance and labor rights: Codes of conduct and anti-sweatshop struggles in global apparel factories in Mexico and Guatemala." *Politics & Society* 33(2), 203–333.

Ryan, T. (2013). *Experts: Bangladesh accord is a game changer.* http://www.solidaritycenter.org/content.asp?contentid=1716 (accessed 7 January 2016).

Salido Marcos, J. and T. Bellhouse. 2016. "Economic and social upgrading: Definitions, connections and exploring means of measurement." Sede Subregional de la CEPAL en México (Estudios e Investigaciones) 40096, Naciones Unidas Comisión Económica para América Latina y el Caribe (CEPAL).

Samaddar, K. K. (2016). "Occupational health and safety management in RMG sector of Bangladesh." *International Journal of Scientific and Technology Research* 5(12), pp. 176–193.

Santoro, M. (2000). *Profits and principles.* Ithaca, NY: Cornell University Press.

Scheper, C. (2017). "Labour networks under supply chain capitalism: The politics of the Bangladesh accord." *Development and Change* 48(5), 1069–1088.

Schüßler, E., S. Frenkel, S. Ashwin, N. Kabeer, N. Egels-Zandén, R. Alexander, L. Huq, C. Oka, N. Lohmeyer, S. Rahman and K. M. Rahman. (2019). *Garment supply chains since Rana Plaza: Governance and worker outcomes.* Garment Supply Chain Governance Project Final Report.

Shipar, M. (2017). Steps taken by Ministry of Labor and Employment and other related stakeholders after Rana Plaza collapse at Savar. https://cpd.org.bd/wp-content/uploads/2016/04/Presentation-of-Mr-Mikail-Shipar-Secretary-Ministry-of-Labour-and-Employment.pdf (accessed 12 January 2018).

Siddiqi, H. G. A. (2004). *The readymade garment industry of Bangladesh.* Dhaka: The University Press limited.

Siddiqui, T. (2003). "Migration as a livelihood strategy of the poor: The Bangladesh case." Paper presented at the regional conference on migration, development and pro-poor policy choices in Asia. Dhaka, Bangladesh.

Smith, S. (2003). *The multi fibre arrangement—A thread of protectionism.* http://econserv2.bess.tcd.ie/SER/1998/Essay21.htm (accessed 10 July 2005).

Sobhan, R. (2014). *Bangladesh's disaster: Perspectives on the political economy.* http://cpd.org.bd/bangladeshs-disaster-perspectives-on-the-political-economy-rehman-sobhan/ (accessed 19 March 2014).

Stiglitz, J. E. (1999). "The World Bank at the millennium." *The Economic Journal* 109(November), 577–597.

Suhrawardi, R. (2020). "Collapse of Bangladesh's garment industry during coronavirus leaves its workers more vulnerable than ever." *Forbes.* March 30, 2020. https://www.forbes.com/sites/rebeccasuhrawardi/2020/03/30/collapse-of-bangladeshs-garment-industry-leaves-its-workers-more-vulnerable-than-ever-during--coronavirus/#2afd9ccaf27e.

Sweezy, P. M. (1968). *The theory of capitalist development: Principles of Marxian political economy.* New York: Modern Reader Paperbacks.

Taplin, I. M. (2014). "Who is to blame? A re-examination of fast fashion after the 2013 factory disaster in Bangladesh." *Critical Perspectives on International Business* 10(1/2), 72–83.

Textile Today. (2020). "133 RMG units shut down in 2019." *Textile Today*. 12 January. https://www.textiletoday.com.bd/133-rmg-units-shut-2019/

The Bureau of Economic and Business Affairs. (2000). *1999 Country reports on economic policy and trade practices.*

The Daily Star. (1994). "Election funding from businessman." February 27, 1994.

The Daily Star. (2006). "Bank default." June 6, 2006.

The Daily Star. (2010). "26 killed in factory fire." December 15, 2010. https://www.thedailystar.net/news-detail-166145.

The Daily Star. (2016). "BGMEA rejects TIB report." January 15, 2020. https://www.thedailystar.net/country/bgmea-rejects-tib-report-202369.

The Daily Star. (2017). EU finds fantastic progress under sustainability compact. https://www.thedailystar.net/business/eu-finds-fantastic-progress-under-sustainability-compact-1402675. May 9.

The Daily Star. (2019). "BGMEA building set to be demolished this week." October 21, 2019. https://www.thedailystar.net/city/news/bgmea-building-set-be-demolished-week-1816501.

The Daily Star. (2020). "BGMEA issues reopen timetable." 26 April 2020. https://www.thedailystar.net/frontpage/news/bgmea-issues-reopen-timetable-1896880.

The Dawn. (1956). *The Dawn*. 9 January 1956.

The Economist Intelligence Unit [EIU]. (1999). *The Economist Intelligence Unit (EIU). (2002/2003/2005). "Country report: Bangladesh."* London: Redhouse Press Ltd.

The Telegraph. (2020). *Amartya Sen draws comparison with Bangladesh. October 27, 2020.* https://www.telegraphindia.com/west-bengal/amartya-sen-draws-comparison-with-bangladesh/cid/1749922.

Tobin, L. (2013), "Dhaka factory tragedy fails to deter Primark shoppers." *Evening Standard*, 11 July, p. 46.

Transparency International Bangladesh. (2013). *Readymade garments sector: Problems of good governance and way forward.* https://blog.transparency.org/wp-content/uploads/2014/04/2013_TIB_GarmentSector_EN.pdf.

Trela, I. and J. Whalley. (1990). "Unravelling the threads of the MFA." In C. B. Hamilton (Ed.), *Textiles trade and the developing countries: Eliminating the multi-fibre arrangement in the 1990s.* Washington, DC: The World Bank.

Uddin, G. S. (2008). "Wage productivity and wage income differential in labor market: Evidence from RMG sector in Bangladesh." *Asian Social Science*, 4(12), 92–101.

Uddin, M. (2020a). "Time to put workers first." *The Daily Star*. https://www.thedailystar.net/opinion/rmg-notes/news/time-put-workers-first-1929269.

Uddin, M. (2020b). "Garments industry needs evolution, not revolution." *The Daily Star*. June 20, 2020. https://www.thedailystar.net/opinion/rmg-notes/news/garments-industry-needs-evolution-not-revolution-1921957.

Uddin, M. (2020c). "Global suppliers are stronger working together." *The Daily Star*. 2020. https://www.thedailystar.net/opinion/rmg-notes/news/global-suppliers-are-stronger-working-together-1914321.

Wallerstein, I. (1987). *World-System analysis.* Stanford, CA: Stanford University Press.

Westergaard, K. (1983). "Rural pauperisation: Its impact on the economic role and status of rural women in Bangladesh." In J. Huq, H. Begum, K. Salahuddin and S. R. Qadir (Eds.), *Women in Bangladesh: Some socio-economic issues* (pp. 17–35). Dhaka: Women for Women.

Woodruff, C. (2014). "Managing for efficiency in the garment sector." In D. Willem te Velde (Ed.), *Enhancing productivity in Bangladesh's garment sector*. Current policy and research debates by DEGRP, UK. pp. 13–14.

World Bank. (2018). Bangladesh data. https://data.worldbank.org/indicator/SP.POP.GROW?locations=BD.

Zafarullah, H. (2003). "Globalisation, state and politics in Bangladesh: Implications for democratic governance." *South Asia: Journal of South Asian Studies* 26(3), 283–296.

Zaman, H. (2001). "Paid work and socio-political consciousness of garment workers in Bangladesh." *Journal of Contemporary Asia* 31(2), 145–159.

Zohir, S. C. and P. Paul-Majumder. (1996). "Garment workers in Bangladesh: Economic, social and health conditions." Research Monograph No. 18. Dhaka: BIDS.

Index

Note: **Bold** page numbers refer to tables; *italic* page numbers refer to figures; page numbers followed by "n" denote endnotes.

absence of staff amenities 30
absenteeism 53, **57**, 61, **67**, 79
Accord 15, *19*, 41, 47–48, 60–61, **67**, 68, 72, 78–79, 82–9, 91, 94–8, 100, 108, 111, 128–129, 132
accountability 84
adverse working conditions 30, 32, 113
Air Raid Precautions 112
Akhtar, N. 122
Alliance 15, *19*, 41, 47, 60–61, 72, 78–79, 82–7, 88, 90–3, 100, 108, 111, 128–129, 132
Amin, S. 25–26, 35
Anner, M. 30, 82, 107, 112, 116, 122, 131
anti-sweatshop 106
article 22 95
artisan class 2–3
asymmetric power 93, 97, 100, 131
audit 31, 47, **57**, 61, 79–80, 87, 100, 106–110, 121
auditing 84, 107–110
Auto Fire-off Ball 85
automated operation 40
automation 60, 75–76, 103, 128, 133

Bangladesh Garment Manufacturer and Exporter Association 15
Bangladesh National Building Code 84, 86
Bangladesh RMG 14–15, 19, 22, 30, 40–2, 76, 78, 98, 100–101, 106, 108, 116–117, **118**, 122, 125, 129, 131–132
Bantai 50–7, 62
bargaining power 110, 113, 129
"behind schedule" 89
Benefits for Business and Workers 118
Bengal 2, 12–13
better price 112
better work 102, 118, 121
bonus 50–51, 75, 103–104
BRAC 10, 12, 84
brands 21, 48, 66, 82–5, 94, 97, 106, 112, 114–115, 122, 124–125, 130, 132–133
building safety 41, 47, 77, 79, 82, 85, 87–90, 128
bureaucratic problems 34
business case 118, 121, 130
Business Social Compliance Initiative 107
business sustainability 40, 100, 130
business value 37
buyer-driven 116
buyer-supplier relationship 115, 131

capacity building 77, 80, **118**, 119, 130
complaint boxes 68
compliance score 70
capitalist class 5
capitalist endeavour 40
capturing state power 45
cheap labour 101, 106
Clean by Design 118
Clean Clothes Campaign 46, 82–83
code of conduct 31, **57**, 80, 88, 100, 108, 110, 114, 121
"coercive compliance" 97–98
collaboration 16–8, 48, 85, 115, 131, 133
comparative advantages 41
competitive 42–43, 62, 76, 78, 80, 86, 97, 106, 112, 116–117, 129
compliant 41, 50, 95, 97, 103–104, 112, 129
contract-based workers 58, 67
corporate business models 100, 112

corporate career 38
corrective action plans 83, 96
corruption 5, 47, 89
COVID-19 15, 122, 124–125, 133
"cream" factories 130
CSR **61**, 84–85, 88, 107, 111, 115
culture 12, 23, 36, 42, 45, 63, 73, 85, 102, 104, 132
culture of safety 85, 132

Daewoo 16–17
day-care 52, 62
DEA 85, 90–2, 94
decentralization 6
democratic culture 45
dependency on aid 11
dependency ratio 8
Desh 16–8, 39
detailed engineering assessment 99n8
"development model" 2
DIFE 47–48, 77, 84, 86, 129
disadvantaged group 53
"divide and rule" 133
division of labour 23
domestic responsibilities 24
double payment 51
duplication 107, 111, 130

East Bengal 2–3, 13
East Pakistan 2–4, 13
economic dispossession 3
economic upgrading 116–117
efficiency incentive 69
efficiency rates 101
Eid 51, 59
elite middle class 35
empowerment 10, 12, 26, 36, 40, 83, 127, 129
entrepreneur class 1, 129
entrepreneurs 1, 4–5, 17, 34–35, 38, 40–41, 45, 55, 77, 85–86, 97–98, 106, 130, 133
Enterprise Resource Planning 74
'ethically deficient' 96
ethical price 113
Everything But Arms 21, 78
export-processing zone 6

family-based living 26
fast-fashion 106, 114, 116
female labour 23–24, 128
fertility rate 8
financial security 24
fire doors 85, 87–88, 94
first-generation entrepreneurs 34
force majeure 122, 125, 133
foreign staffs 76
freedom of association 46, 107

gender-based approach 101
Gender Embedded Index 117
General Agreement of Tariff and Trade 14
Generalised System Preferences 82
Generalized Scheme of Preferences 20–21
globalization 33, 56, 116
global labour standard 41, 129
global production network 30
global supply chain 41, 97–98, 100, 112, 116, 128
global value chains 116
governmental policy 34
government patronage 45–46
Grameen Bank 10, 12

health and safety committee 30, 31, 83
health programme 52
healthy work environment 50
HER 118–20
hidden cost 29
high road 65, 80
human rights 78, 114

ILO 48, 78, 83–84, 86, 95, 103, 106–107, **118**, 128
importers 20
import-substituting industrialization 4
inclusive growth 127
income inequality 127
IndustriALL and UNi Global Union 82
industrial democracy 84
industrial disaster 29
industrial engineers 39
industrialization 2, 4, 7–9, 16, 35, 130
industrial relations **118**, 132
inequality 23, 127
infant mortality 9
initiatives 12, 31, 41, 44, 77, 84–6, 88, 94, 97, 100, 106, 111, 115–9, 121, 128–1
"innovative work" 65
inspections 78, 82, 83, 87–90, 97–98, 107
international basket case 1

joint-venture company 35, 50
jute mills 13

Kabeer, N. 2, 22–4, 30, 102, 111
knit 19, **67**

LDC 12, 16, 20, 78
labour-driven 100

labour efficiency 71
labour-intensive 8, 11
labour management 132
labour organizations 59, 82
labour productivity **61**, 71, 75, 100–2, 104–6
labour standards 30, 46, 66, 106–107, 112, 121
labour turnover 61, 67–68, 79, 102
lead time 101, 106, 112, 115
Lean Retaining 114
"learning by doing" 97
learning curve 106
least developed countries 15
legislation 77
Letters of Credit 17
liberalization 4, 7–8
living wage 32
loan defaults 46
lower middle-income country 1–2, 12, 78, 127

male-dominated society 26, 53
management approach 74
management perception 128
management strategy 59, 73, 75, 102, 105
Management Training Unit 74
management-worker relation 61–62, 67, 79
maternity leave 30–31, 51, 68
mass production 128
Member of Parliament 45
micro-credit 9–10
mid-level management 28, 58, 60, 62–63, 74–6, 80, 102, 105
migration 10–2, 25–26, 32, 102, 104, 130
minimum wage 30–2, 47, 105, 126
monthly production 54
motivate 75, 103–104, 130
Multi-fibre Arrangement 14
multipurpose buildings 92, 128
multi-stakeholder 48, 85, 94, 108
multi-stakeholder governance 108
multi-stakeholder initiatives 94
muslin 2
mutual gains 65

National Initiative 41, 47, 60, 111, 132
nationalization 4–5
National Occupational Safety and Health Policy 77
new generation 35, 38, 41–42
New Industrial Policy 6
Newly Industrialized Countries 16
NGO 24, 35–36, 52
non-compliant factory 57
non-productive time 104

occupational hazards 30
occupational safety and health 77, 101
off-peak time 106
overtime 31, 51, 56, 59, 61, 67, 79, 93, 104–105, 108, 110

PaCT 63, 118–119
paid employment 23, 25
paid labour market 22–23, 127
Pakistan 1, 3–4, 10, 13, 127
pandemic 122, 124–125, 133
participation of women 23, 27, 127–9
partition 3, 13
patronize 73
philanthropy 132
piece-rate workers 59, 104
politics 27–28, 46, 58, 75, 80
poor wages 30, 38
population growth 8, **9**, 26
poverty 7–8, 10–11, 22–23, 133
private and public 108
private regulatory 48
privatization 5–7
production costs 101
production manager **57**, 58–60, 75
productivity 42, 50, 54, **61**, 65, 71, 75, 100–2, 104–6, 110–111, 117, 120, 130
professionalism 57, 63, 73, 102, 104, 130
professional human resources 40
professional mentality 104
profitability 50, 53, 55, 117
profit margin 41, 72, 80, 112, 114
purchasing practices 100, 107, 111–112, 114

Quick Response 114
quotas 14–6, 20

Rana Plaza 15, 18–19, 27, 29, 31, 41, 47, 72, 77–78, 82–83, 85–7, 93, 97–98, 100, 107–108, 111–112, 128–129, 131
rate of rejection 54
rejection rate 75, 104
relocation 92, 111, 128
remediation 48, 77–9, 83, 87, 89–90, 92, 94–8, 100, 111, 129, 131–132
remittance **9**, 10–11, 23, 127
Review panel 92
rights of workers 50
RMG industry 11, 14–6, 18–19, 29, 73, 76, 83, 98, 100, 106, 108, 117, 126–127, 132

RMG Sustainability Council 15, 47, 131
rental power plant 45
respected professions 35
responsible business 122
retailers 21, 82, 92, 114–115, 122, 125, 129, 131–132
retrofitting 89–90
rural development 5, 10

"safe investment" 41
safety compliances 18, 97
safety of workers 29, 103
scalability 118, 121
second-generation entrepreneurs 35, 38, 41
self-sufficiency in rice 9
shared responsibility 80, 94, 96, 108, 131, 132
signatory companies 91, 95
skilled labour 10
skilled management 132
skilled workers 41, 103–104
social audits 107
social clause 106
social compliance 82, 85, **115**, 130
social control 26, 65–66
social cost 30
social development 12, 54, 127
social distancing 122
social impact 22, 26
socialist economy 4
social upgrading 101, 116–117
societal status 24–25
solidarity of suppliers 115, 133
sordid mentality 104
sprinkler 86, 94
squeezer machine 57
squeezing of prices 111, 116
state-controlled economy 4
stimulus package 125–126, 133
stringent terms and conditions of garment employment 30
Structural Adjustment Programmes 7
structural, fire and electric safety 100, 131
structural problem 103
structural safety 41, 84–6, 91, 132
subcontracting 47, **61**, 62
subcontractor 37, 62, 129
subsistence 32
supervisors 51, 58–59, 69, 75, 101–102, 105
sustainable 41, 100, 106, **118**, 121, 129–130, 133
sustainable business 126n2
sustainability 15, 41, 47, 63, 74, 85, 100, 106, 109, 116–117, 119, 121, 130–131, 133
"sustainability compact" 78
Sweden Textile Water Initiative 118

tariff 7, 18
tax holiday 7
Tazreen 29, 82
Tazreen Garments 29
third-party audit system 31
Time and Action 74
top management 58, 67, 70, 73, 75, 80, 105
traditional CSR 88
trade-friendly policy 17
trade liberalization policy 4, 8
trade union(s) 24, 29, 31, 48, 77, 82, 83, 85, 107, 114
traditional mindset 38
training centre 69, 75, 103
transparency 18, 75, 84, 86, 126
training 15, 17, 30, 44, 59, 61–62, 69, 74–75, 77, 79–80, 83–84, 101–4, **118**, 120–121, 130
transnational governance 41, 78, 82, 87, 97–98, 100, 112, 128
turnover 53, **57**, 61, 65–66, **67**, 68, 79, 102, 104, 130
turnover rate 53, 104

unified code of conduct 88, 108, 110
unethical practices 114
upgrading 83, 100–2, 115–7, 121
Utilization Declaration 46

vulnerability 32–33, 50, 71–72, 113, 122

wages 27, 29–30, 38, 51, 53, **57**, 65, 67, 79, 93, 103, 107, 112–4, 116, *125*, 126, 133
weak state 45
welfare programmes 52–5, 62, 103, 130
Woo-Choong, K. 16
workers' health 30
worker safety 82, 89, 128
Workers Participation Committee 67
workers' rights 15, 79, 107, 112
workplace(s) 29–30, 35, 41, 50, 52, 56–8, 61–62, 65–66, 68, 73–5, 78–80, 85, 87, 89, 93, 103, 105, 113, 114, **118**, 121, 129
workplace safety 41, 61, 85
workplace stress 30
woven 19

For Product Safety Concerns and Information please contact our EU representative GPSR@taylorandfrancis.com
Taylor & Francis Verlag GmbH, Kaufingerstraße 24, 80331 München, Germany

www.ingramcontent.com/pod-product-compliance
Lightning Source LLC
LaVergne TN
LVHW021130300926
849160LV00010B/941
9780367720520